Test it

FCE: Use of English

Upper-intermediate

Kenna Bourke
and Amanda Maris

OXFORD
UNIVERSITY PRESS

OXFORD

UNIVERSITY PRESS

Great Clarendon Street, Oxford OX2 6DP

Oxford University Press is a department of the University of Oxford.
It furthers the University's objective of excellence in research, scholarship,
and education by publishing worldwide in

Oxford New York

Auckland Cape Town Dar es Salaam Hong Kong Karachi
Kuala Lumpur Madrid Melbourne Mexico City Nairobi
New Delhi Shanghai Taipei Toronto

With offices in

Argentina Austria Brazil Chile Czech Republic France Greece
Guatemala Hungary Italy Japan Poland Portugal Singapore
South Korea Switzerland Thailand Turkey Ukraine Vietnam

OXFORD and OXFORD ENGLISH are registered trade marks of
Oxford University Press in the UK and in certain other countries

ISBN-13: 978 0 19 439207 5
ISBN-10: 0 19 439207 4

Printed in Spain by Unigraf S.L.

Contents

How to use *Test it, Fix it*

Test it, Fix it is a series of books designed to help you identify any problems you may have in English, and to fix the problems. This book contains four tests on each of the five parts of the FCE Use of English paper (paper 3).

Test it, Fix it has an unusual format. You start at the **first** page of each unit, then go to the **third** page, then to the **second** page. Here's how it works:

Test it (First page)

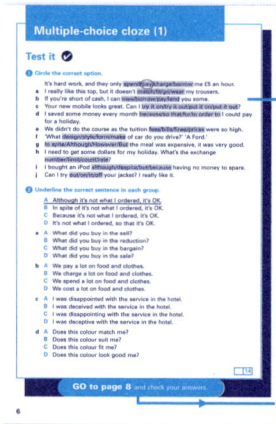

1 Do the exercises on the *Test it* page. In this book, these exercises will help you prepare for the exam format task on the *Test it again* page.

2 Go to the *Fix it* page and check your answers before you do *Test it again*.

Fix it (Third page)

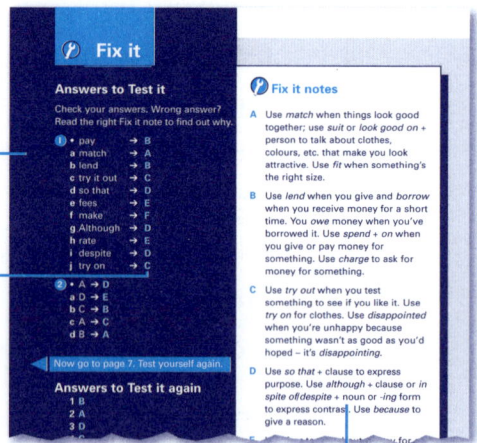

3 Check your answers. You can fold the page to make it easier to check.

4 Wrong answer? Look for the *Fix it note* letter you need.

5 To understand why you made a mistake, read the *Fix it note*. If you need more information, read the *Review* page as well.

6 Now go back to the second page and do *Test it again*.

Test it again (Second page)

7 Do the exercise on the *Test it again* page.

8 Go to the *Fix it* page and check your answers.

Fix it (Third page)

9 Check your answers.

Review (Fourth page)

10 You can read this page at any time. It gives you extended *Fix it* notes and examples. It's designed to give you a summary of the information you need for the whole test.

Test it ✔

1 **Circle the correct option.**

It's hard work, and they only spend/pay/charge/borrow me £5 an hour.

a   I really like this top, but it doesn't match/fit/go/wear my trousers.

b   If you're short of cash, I can owe/borrow/pay/lend you some.

c   Your new mobile looks great. Can I try it on/try it out/put it on/put it out?

d   I saved some money every month because/so that/for/in order to I could pay for a holiday.

e   We didn't do the course as the tuition fees/bills/fines/prices were so high.

f   'What design/style/form/make of car do you drive?' 'A Ford.'

g   In spite/Although/However/But the meal was expensive, it was very good.

h   I need to get some dollars for my holiday. What's the exchange number/limit/count/rate?

i   I bought an iPod although/despite/but/because having no money to spare.

j   Can I try out/on/in/off your jacket? I really like it.

2 **Underline the correct sentence in each group.**

A   Although it's not what I ordered, it's OK.
B   In spite of it's not what I ordered, it's OK.
C   Because it's not what I ordered, it's OK.
D   It's not what I ordered, so that it's OK.

a   A   What did you buy in the sell?
B   What did you buy in the reduction?
C   What did you buy in the bargain?
D   What did you buy in the sale?

b   A   We pay a lot on food and clothes.
B   We charge a lot on food and clothes.
C   We spend a lot on food and clothes.
D   We cost a lot on food and clothes.

c   A   I was disappointed with the service in the hotel.
B   I was deceived with the service in the hotel.
C   I was disappointing with the service in the hotel.
D   I was deceptive with the service in the hotel.

d   A   Does this colour match me?
B   Does this colour suit me?
C   Does this colour fit me?
D   Does this colour look good me?

14

GO to page 8 and check your answers.

Test it again ✔

Read the text below and decide which answer (A, B, C or D) best fits each space.

SPEND, SPEND, SPEND

People's attitude to money has changed in recent years. When my mother was younger, she never (1) .... from anyone and she always paid her (2) .... on time. Things like cars, TVs and washing machines (3) .... a huge amount of money and there weren't so many different (4) .... to choose from. Nowadays, the (5) .... of mobile phones on the market is unbelievable. Some of my friends change their mobile every few months (6) .... the expense. There is also huge choice in clothes and shoes, especially on the internet. I ordered some jeans once but they were very (7) .... because they didn't (8) .... me very well – they were much too big. I prefer to try things (9) .... before I buy them. I think I know what (10) .... good on me and I quite often get great (11) .... in the sales. Some shops (12) .... a fortune but the (13) .... of clothes that they sell is awful. They persuade people to buy things that don't (14) .... them, just because they have a designer label. I don't have to pay high (15) .... in shops in order to feel good about the way I look.

	A	B	C	D
1	lent	borrowed	paid	owed
2	bills	fees	prices	limits
3	spent	paid	charged	cost
4	design	style	makes	forms
5	rate	number	limit	count
6	although	despite	however	but
7	deceptive	disappointed	deceived	disappointing
8	fit	match	look	suit
9	out	on	up	through
10	suits	matches	looks	fits
11	bargains	fines	reduction	price
12	cost	charge	owe	borrow
13	form	brands	style	designs
14	suit	match	goes	wear
15	fees	bills	fines	prices

15

Fix it

Answers to Test it

Check your answers. Wrong answer?
Read the right Fix it note to find out why.

1
- pay → **B**
  - **a** match → **A**
  - **b** lend → **B**
  - **c** try it out → **C**
  - **d** so that → **D**
  - **e** fees → **E**
  - **f** make → **F**
  - **g** Although → **D**
  - **h** rate → **E**
  - **i** despite → **D**
  - **j** try on → **C**

2
- A → **D**
  - **a** D → **E**
  - **b** C → **B**
  - **c** A → **C**
  - **d** B → **A**

Now go to page 7. Test yourself again.

Answers to Test it again

1 B
2 A
3 D
4 C
5 B
6 B
7 D
8 A
9 B
10 C
11 A
12 B
13 C
14 A
15 D

Fix it notes

A Use *match* when things look good together; use *suit* or *look good on* + person to talk about clothes, colours, etc. that make you look attractive. Use *fit* when something's the right size.

B Use *lend* when you give and *borrow* when you receive money for a short time. You *owe* money when you've borrowed it. Use *spend* + *on* when you give or pay money for something. Use *charge* to ask for money for something.

C Use *try out* when you test something to see if you like it. Use *try on* for clothes. Use *disappointed* when you're unhappy because something wasn't as good as you'd hoped – it's *disappointing*.

D Use *so that* + clause to express purpose. Use *although* + clause or *in spite of/despite* + noun or *-ing* form to express contrast. Use *because* to give a reason.

E Use *fees* to talk about money for a professional service; a *bill* is a request for payment. A *rate* is a fixed amount of money that you pay. A *sale* is a period when things are cheaper than usual, and a *bargain* is an item at a reduced price.

F Use *make* to talk about a product made by a particular company.

For more information, see the Review page opposite.

ⓘ Review

- In part 1 of paper 3 read the title and the text through first to get an idea of the content. Don't look at the options, A–D.
- Read the text again carefully, focusing on the whole sentence around each gap, not just the words that follow.

See page 86 for a description of this part of the Use of English paper.

Clothing and appearance You use the verb *match* when something looks good with something else, especially when you're talking about clothes. You use *suit* or *look good on* + person to talk about clothes, colours, etc. that make a person look attractive. You use *fit* when something's the right size.
I must buy some shoes to match my skirt.
That style looks very good on you, and the colour really suits you.
My jeans don't fit me any more.

Buying things You use *try out* when you test something to see if you like it. Note that when you put clothes or shoes on in a shop to see if they fit you, you use *try on* (not *try out*).
Can it try out this camera before I buy it?
I never buy anything without trying it on.

You use *disappointed* to say that you're unhappy because something wasn't as good as you'd hoped. The object, service, etc. is *disappointing*.
I bought a video camera on the net but I was very disappointed with the quality.
The quality of the camera was very disappointing.

⚠ Don't confuse *disappointed* with *deceived*. If someone or something deceives you, they or it make you think that something that's false is true.
The shop deceived its customers by selling T-shirts with false designer labels.

Money You use *lend* when you give money to someone for a short time and *borrow* when someone gives you money for a short time. This is money you give back to the other person. You *owe* money when you've borrowed it.
I need to borrow some money. Can you lend me $50?
We owe the bank thousands of dollars.

You use *spend + on* when you give or pay money for something. You use *charge* to ask for money for an object or service.
I spend most of my salary on rent.
They charged me a fortune for a salad!

You use *fees* to talk about money you pay for a professional service or advice. Note that *fee* can be singular or plural. You use *rate* to talk about a fixed amount of money that you pay and you use *price* to describe what something costs. A *bill* is a request for payment, e.g. *gas bill, restaurant bill.*
They paid me a fee of £500 for the report.
The rate of interest is very low.
What's the price of this vase?

A *sale* is a period when things are cheaper than usual, and a *bargain* is an item at a reduced price, or something that's very good value.
How many bargains did you get in the sale?

Makes and styles You use *make* to talk about a product made by a particular company. You use *style* to talk about the form or look of something.
'What make of jeans are those?' 'Levi's.'
That style of jeans really suits you.

So that You use *so that* + clause to say why you do something.
I'm waiting until the sales so that I can pick up some bargains. (because I want to pick up some bargains)

Although and in spite of You use *although* + clause or *in spite of/despite* + noun or *-ing* form to express contrast. You often use these words before a clause that makes the main clause seem surprising.
Although I was late, I still caught the bus.
Despite the cost, Jill bought a new car.

Because You use *because* to give a reason.
I'm happy because you're here.

Test it ✓

1 **Circle the correct option.**

Mark has applied to/~~for~~/by fifty jobs so far without success.
a   It's a bad idea to depend from/on/of other people all the time.
b   I can see that you don't approve about/for/of what I'm doing.
c   Does Joanna believe in/with/for the paranormal?
d   Why don't you agree with/in/about me?
e   Helen is married for/with/to Stephen.

2 **Circle the correct option, A or B.**

Jo .... her sister next weekend.
A visits   **B** is visiting
a   Nobody .... Jack lately. He must have gone away somewhere.
   A has seen   **B** saw
b   Katya .... cry a lot when she was a small child.
   A did   **B** used to
c   John .... Dr Denny tomorrow at 10.45.
   A is seeing   **B** sees
d   By the time Francis is four, he .... read.
   A can   **B** will be able to
e   Don't panic! I'll .... to him by the time you get here.
   A have spoken   **B** speak
f   The town of Nai Nital stands .... a lake in the Himalayas.
   A on   **B** in
g   What Tim likes most is going ....
   A to fish   **B** fishing
h   Every day, the old man .... out for a walk.
   A goes   **B** is going
i   Sometimes we all have to force .... to smile.
   A ourselves   **B** us
j   Grandpa always wanted a little place .... the sea.
   A on   **B** by
k   By the time she .... telling the joke, everyone's usually asleep.
   A finished   **B** 's finished
l   Did you .... to discos when you were a teenager?
   A use to go   **B** went
m   The boys all went .... in the Sierra Nevada mountains last summer.
   A to hike   **B** hiking

18

GO to page 12 and check your answers.

Test it again ✔

**Read the text below and think of the word which best fits each space.
Use only one word in each space.**

WHERE DID YOU SAY YOU WERE GOING AGAIN?

What (1) .... happened to holidays in recent years? In the past
people (2) .... to enjoy two weeks (3) .... the sea
in July or August. They would stay in a small, family-run hotel, lie on the
beach every day, and relax. Nowadays holidays are about activities and
competition.

Every time I ask certain friends, 'Where (4) .... you going on
holiday this year?', it (5) .... them half an hour to explain. 'This
year we thought we would (6) .... trekking in Peru or diving in
Mauritius. Of course, it depends (7) .... the children. If they go
to summer camp in the US, they (8) .... be able to go to South
America as well. We could also go to our second home in Spain. They
(9) .... have finished building it in July. What about you?'

By the time they (10) .... finished, I still don't know what their
plans are. I force (11) .... to reply, 'I'm staying in a caravan
(12) .... the south coast of England. I don't believe
(13) .... going abroad every year. I don't approve
(14) .... the noise and pollution created (15) ....
air travel and I enjoy discovering my own country.' I'm never sure if they
believe me or not.

15

⚙ Fix it

Answers to Test it

Check your answers. Wrong answer?
Read the right Fix it note to find out why.

1 • for → G
  a on → G
  b of → G
  c in → G
  d with → G
  e to → G

2 • B → A   g B → E
  a A → B   h A → A
  b B → D   i A → F
  c A → A   j B → G
  d B → C   k B → B
  e A → C   l A → D
  f A → G   m B → E

◀ Now go to page 11. Test yourself again.

Answers to Test it again

1 has
2 used
3 by
4 are
5 takes
6 go
7 on
8 won't/will not
9 'll/will
10 've/have
11 myself
12 on
13 in
14 of
15 by

⚙ Fix it notes

A Use the present continuous to talk about future plans and arrangements. Use the present simple to talk about routines and habits.

B Use the present perfect to talk about events that have happened recently and that have an effect in the present, especially with words like *lately*, *recently*.

C Remember that there isn't a future form of the modal verb *can*. Use *will/won't be able to* instead. Use *will have* + past participle to talk about things that will be finished by a particular time in the future.

D Use *used to* to talk about past habits and states that no longer happen in the present.

E You often use an *-ing* form after the verb *go*, especially when you're talking about outdoor sports and activities.

F Use reflexive pronouns, e.g. *myself*, *ourselves* when the subject and object of the verb are the same person.

G Many verbs are often followed by a preposition, e.g. *approve of*. You need to learn these as you go along. Use *by* when you mean 'at the side of' something; use *on* to talk about a position by a lake, sea or ocean.

For more information, see the Review page opposite. ▷

ℹ️ **Review**

- In part 2 of paper 3 read the title and the text through first to get an idea of the content. Don't try to fill in any of the gaps.
- Decide on the type of word you need (verb, preposition, etc.) before you fill in each gap.

See page 86 for a description of this part of the Use of English paper.

Present simple and continuous You use the present continuous to talk about future plans and arrangements. You use the present simple to talk about routines and habits.
I'm going on holiday next week.
I go on holiday twice a year.

⚠️ Don't use present continuous to talk about routines and habits.
I see my friends every weekend.
NOT *I'm seeing my friends every weekend.*

Present perfect You use the present perfect to talk about events that have happened recently and that have an effect in the present, especially with words like *lately* or *recently*.
I've been very busy recently.
Have you seen your family lately?

Will be able to Remember that there isn't a future form of the modal verb *can*, so you use *will/won't be able to* instead.
In the future everyone will be able to work and study from home.

Future perfect You use *will have* + past participle to talk about things that will be finished by a particular time in the future. You can use *by* + time and *by the time* (*that*) + present with this structure.
I'll have finished the report by 5.00.
We'll have landed by the time you finish work.

Used to You use *used to* to talk about past habits and states that no longer happen in the present. Don't confuse this with *be used to* which means 'be accustomed to' and can be used to talk about the present.
I used to wear glasses but I have contact lenses now.
I'm used to getting up early every day.

Go + -ing You often use an *-ing* form after the verb *go*, especially when you're talking about outdoor sports and activities. You don't repeat *go* after *going to*.
I go skating every weekend.
I'm going walking next week.
NOT *I'm going to go walking next week.*

Reflexive pronouns You use reflexive pronouns, e.g. *myself, ourselves*, when the subject and object of the verb are the same person.
We bought ourselves a new car last month.

Verb + preposition Many verbs are often followed by a preposition, e.g. *approve of, belong to*. Try to make a note of these verbs and learn them as you go along.
I don't approve of smoking.
Who does this dog belong to?

Prepositions of place You use *by* to mean 'at the side of' something, e.g. *by the house, by the desk*. You use *on* to talk about a position by a lake, sea or ocean.
Please leave the boxes by the door.
We're renting a cottage on the lake.

Test it ✔

1 **Look at the words in bold in a–k. Then match them to a similar meaning in 1–11.**

a	**If it stopped raining**, we'd go outside.	1 who does it belong to?	a ....2....
b	I **take after** my mum.	2 it's raining now	b ....
c	Nick has lived in Cairo **since 2004**.	3 it's a good idea	c ....
d	We **didn't bring** the guidebook with us.	4 collect	d ....
e	You've **never** been to Hong Kong, have you?	5 not once	e ....
f	Mandy really **ought to** see a doctor about that.	6 resemble	f ....
g	Paul **had better not** call his girlfriend – she's furious.	7 it wouldn't be a good idea	g ....
h	**Whose** sports car is that?	8 for a few years	h ....
i	**If I were you**, I'd emigrate.	9 it would be fun	i ....
j	I'll **pick** you **up** at eight.	10 left behind	j ....
k	**I'd like to** listen to more live jazz if I had time.	11 should	k ....

2 **Does sentence B mean the same as sentence A?**

			SAME	DIFFERENT
	A Stu's cut down on cigarettes.	B Stu doesn't smoke as much as before.	☑	☐
a	A You'd better not be lying.	B I hope you're telling the truth.	☐	☐
b	A Whose car is that?	B Who's driving that car?	☐	☐
c	A I can't find my tablets.	B I've lost my tablets.	☐	☐
d	A It's ages since we last saw you.	B We haven't seen you for ages.	☐	☐
e	A Pat had never seen so much snow.	B It was the most snow Pat had ever seen.	☐	☐
f	A You ought to take the dog to the vet's.	B You've arranged to take the dog to the vet's.	☐	☐
g	A I wouldn't work if I were rich.	B If I wasn't poor, I wouldn't work.	☐	☐
h	A I've run out of time.	B I haven't got any time left.	☐	☐
i	A I haven't ever eaten snails.	B I'll never eat snails.	☐	☐
j	A Keith always forgets his wife's birthday.	B Keith never remembers his wife's birthday.	☐	☐

20

GO to page 16 and check your answers.

Test it again ✔

Complete the second sentence so that it has a similar meaning to the first sentence, using the word given. Do not change the word given. You must use between two and five words, including the word given.

1 There's isn't any bread left.
   run
   We .... bread.

2 You haven't visited Mum and Dad for weeks.
   since
   It's weeks .... Mum and Dad.

3 The baby really resembles his grandfather.
   after
   The baby .... his grandfather.

4 You ought to see a dentist about that tooth.
   were
   If I .... a dentist about that tooth.

5 'Whose is that fantastic car?' she asked.
   belong
   'Who .... to?' she asked

6 I can't remember anything he said.
   have
   I .... he said.

7 It wouldn't be a good idea to make him angry.
   better
   You .... make him angry.

8 It would be nice to work for myself; then I'd have more freedom.
   worked
   If .... for myself, I'd have more freedom.

9 We last went abroad in 2005.
   been
   We .... 2005.

10 That's the best meal I've ever eaten.
   never
   I .... such a good meal.

20

Fix it

Answers to Test it

Check your answers. Wrong answer?
Read the right Fix it note to find out why.

1
- a 2 → D
- b 6 → F
- c 8 → A
- d 10 → G
- e 5 → B
- f 11 → C
- g 7 → C
- h 1 → E
- i 3 → C
- j 4 → F
- k 9 → D

2
- • same → F
- a same → C
- b different → E
- c same → G
- d same → A
- e same → B
- f different → C
- g same → D
- h same → F
- i different → B
- j same → G

Now go to page 15. Test yourself again.

Answers to Test it again

(2 marks for each correct sentence)
1 've/have run out of
2 since you visited
3 really takes after
4 were you I'd see
5 does that fantastic car belong
6 've/have forgotten everything
7 'd/had better not
8 I worked
9 haven't been abroad since
10 've/have never eaten

Fix it notes

A Use *for* with present perfect to talk about a period of time, e.g. *for three days*. Use *since* to say when the period started, e.g. *since 2005*. *Last* + past simple means the same as the negative form of present perfect + *for* or *since*.

B Use the adverbs *ever* and *never* with the present perfect and past perfect to talk about experiences in your life. Use *ever* in questions. Use *never* in positive sentences.

C Use *If I were you, you ought to* and *you should* to give someone advice. You can also use *had better (not)* to say what you think someone should do.

D In second conditional sentences, use past simple in the *if*-clause and *would* + base form in the other clause.

E Use the question word *whose* to ask about possessions. *Whose is this?* means the same as *Who does this belong to?*

F Use phrasal verbs to replace full verbs and in some fixed expressions, e.g. if you run out of something, *there isn't any left*. If you *cut down on something*, you *reduce* it.

G Different verbs can have a very similar meaning but you may need to change positive to negative or negative to positive, e.g. *can't find/lose, forget/not remember, leave behind/not bring*.

For more information, see the Review page opposite.

ⓘ Review

- In part 3 of paper 3 read the first sentence through first. Then read the gapped sentence and decide what is missing.
- Look at the key word and decide how it can be used.

See page 86 for a description of this part of the Use of English paper.

For and since You use *for* with the present perfect to talk about a period of time, e.g. *for three days*. You use *since* to say when the period started, e.g. *since 2005*. This can be a time, date, or event.
I've lived in Spain for five years.
You've been asleep since lunchtime.
They've met twice since the party.

Last + past simple means the same as the negative form of the present perfect + *for* or *since*.
It's Sunday. You last called me on Monday. = You haven't called me for six days/since Monday.

Ever and never You use the adverbs *ever* and *never* with the present perfect and past perfect to talk about experiences in your life. You use *ever* (not *never*) in questions and you use *never* in positive sentences (not in negative sentences).
Have you ever read War and Peace?
My parents have never been abroad.

Giving advice You use *if I were you, you ought to* and *you should* to give someone advice. You can also use *had better (not)* to say what you think someone should do.
If I were you, I'd go to bed early.
You ought to drive more carefully.
You should eat more fresh fruit.
You'd better not phone them after ten.

Second conditional In second conditional sentences, you use the past simple in the *if*-clause and *would* + base form in the other clause. You use the second conditional to talk about unreal situations in the present and unlikely events in the future.
I'd go out with you if I didn't already have a boyfriend. (But I do have one, so I can't.)

If I won a lot of money, I'd give it to charity. (But I probably won't win a lot of money, so I won't give it to charity.)

Whose You use *whose* with or without a noun to ask about possessions. *Whose is this?* means the same as *Who does this belong to?*
Whose mobile is this?
Whose are these?

⚠ Don't confuse *whose* and *who's* (who is/has).
Whose jacket is this?
(Who does it belong to?)
Who's coming to the party?
(Who is coming to the party?)

Phrasal verbs You use phrasal verbs to replace full verbs and some fixed expressions, e.g. if you *run out of* something, there *isn't any left*. If you *cut down on* something, you *reduce* it.
Look up the word in the dictionary. = Find the word in the dictionary.

Negative and positive verbs Different verbs can have a very similar meaning but you may need to change positive to negative or negative to positive, e.g. *can't find/lose, forget/not remember, leave behind/not bring.*
I can't remember his email address. = I've forgotten his email address.

Error correction (1)

Test it ✔

1 Read the sentences. Are the words in bold necessary or unnecessary?

	NECESSARY	UNNECESSARY
She was born on the eighth of ~~the~~ July.	☐	☑
a Many villages **they** have been damaged by last night's storms.	☐	☐
b It was **such** a great party that I didn't want to leave! Thank you!	☐	☐
c I **never** lie because I like to be honest.	☐	☐
d This is much **more** difficult than I thought it would be.	☐	☐
e I really like Philip because he's always **too** happy.	☐	☐
f That's the man who **he** crashed into my car.	☐	☐
g We go **often** to the beach when it's sunny.	☐	☐
h It's a **such** hot day today.	☐	☐
i Are you feeling **more** happier now that you've got a new job?	☐	☐
j The kids are really looking forward to **the** Christmas.	☐	☐

2 Find and cross out ten words in the dialogue that shouldn't be there.

JACK   There you are, at last! You're late ~~always~~! Where have you been? It's already twelve o'clock!

HARRY   Sorry … the bus was more slower than usual and I woke up too late to catch the train. I think it's because it's the Easter. It's always busy on the roads at this time of year.

JACK   Harry, your bus it is always late! Anyway, never mind. We're going to meet Sandra. She's the woman who I met her at Bob's birthday party.

HARRY   The one you fancy? Great. I can't wait to meet her. You talk always about these wonderful people but I never meet them!

JACK   That's not true. Lots of my girlfriends they have met you. Don't you remember Pete and Sam's wedding in the June? There was Carol, and Jane, and Sally, and Pam, and Josie, and …

HARRY   … and Nicola, Sarah, Liz, Helen, Lisa … Yes, you're right. Wow, that was a such fantastic day, wasn't it? Pete looked very happy and Sam looked too beautiful.

JACK   I can't remember. I was having such a good time talking to Victoria that I didn't really notice anyone else. Come on, we'll have to run or we'll be late for the lunch and Sandra won't be happy!

| 20 |

GO to page 20 and check your answers.

Test it again ✔

Read the text and look carefully at each line. Some of the lines are correct, and some have a word that should not be there. If a line is correct, put a tick (✓) next to it. If a line has a word that should not be there, cross it out.

MY BEST YEAR

1   I don't think I'll ever forget being 22. It was an incredible year for me.
2   I've never been more sadder than the day I said goodbye to my
3   family. I had a new job in Australia! It was a such great opportunity that
4   I really couldn't refuse. The job I was going to do there it was for a
5   software company located in Sydney. The salary was fantastic
6   and the people seemed really too nice. So just after my birthday, in
7   the November, I got on a plane and said goodbye to England for
8   the first time. I remember celebrating the Christmas that year. It was such a
9   sunny day! We had a party on the beach. Ted, who it was my new
10   boss, bought lots of champagne and everyone sang traditional Christmas
11   songs. My parents couldn't believe it when I showed them my photos.
12   When I'm at home for Christmas, we go usually to visit my aunt,
13   who's very old now. Mum cooks turkey or goose for the lunch and
14   we exchange presents. Of course it's more colder back home than in
15   Australia! I'll remember always my twenties forever.

15

🔧 Fix it

Answers to Test it

Check your answers. Wrong answer?
Read the right Fix it note to find out why.

1
• unnecessary	→	G
a unnecessary	→	A
b necessary	→	F
c necessary	→	C
d necessary	→	D
e unnecessary	→	E
f unnecessary	→	B
g unnecessary	→	C
h unnecessary	→	F
i unnecessary	→	D
j unnecessary	→	G

2
• late always	→	C
a more slower	→	D
b the Easter	→	G
c it is always	→	A
d I met her	→	B
e talk always	→	C
f girlfriends they	→	A
g in the June	→	G
h a such fantastic	→	F
i too beautiful	→	E
j the lunch	→	G

Now go to page 19. Test yourself again.

Answers to Test it again

1 ✔	9 ~~it~~	
2 ~~more~~	10 ✔	
3 ~~such~~	11 ✔	
4 ~~it~~	12 ~~usually~~	
5 ✔	13 ~~the~~	
6 ~~too~~	14 ~~more~~	
7 ~~the~~	15 ~~always~~	
8 ~~the~~		

🔧 Fix it notes

A Don't use more than one subject in a clause or sentence. Remember that a personal pronoun (*he*, *they*, etc.) can be a subject.

B Don't use more than one subject or object in a relative clause. The relative pronouns *who*, *that*, *which*, etc. replace other pronouns (*he*, *her*, *it*, etc.), so you don't need both.

C Be careful with the position of adverbs. Adverbs of frequency (*always*, *never*, *usually*, etc.) go after full verbs but before the verb *be*.

D Form the comparative of one-syllable adjectives and two-syllable adjectives ending in -*y* by adding -*er*. Don't use *more*. For two-syllable and longer adjectives use *more* + adjective.

E Don't confuse *too* with *very*. *Too* can mean 'more than enough' or 'more than necessary'. Use *too* + adjective or adverb and an infinitive structure, e.g. *It's too early to get up.*

F Use *such ... that* to give an explanation for something. Never use *a such*, use *such a* or leave out *such*.

G Don't use an article with meals, days, months, holidays, special days or festivals.

> For more information, see the Review page opposite. ▷

ℹ️ Review

- In part 4 of paper 3 read the title and the text through first to get an idea of the content. Don't try to spot any extra words.
- Look carefully at each sentence, not just the numbered line.
- The mistakes are extra words which should not be in the sentence. The mistakes are never spelling errors.

See page 86 for a description of this part of the Use of English paper.

Subjects You don't use more than one subject in a clause or sentence. Remember that a personal pronoun (*he*, *they*, etc.) can be a subject.
My mother is a doctor.
NOT *My mother she is a doctor.*

Relative clauses You don't use more than one subject or object in a relative clause. The relative pronouns *who, that, which*, etc. replace other pronouns (*he, her, it*, etc.), so you don't need both.
Vicky is the girl who lives near me.
NOT *Vicky is the girl who she lives near me.*

Adverbs Be careful with the position of adverbs. Adverbs of frequency (*always, never, usually*, etc.) go before full verbs (*go, meet, play*, etc.) but after the verb *be*. In questions, you use adverbs of frequency after an auxiliary + subject.
I usually play tennis on Saturdays.
The city centre is always busy.
Do you usually come to work by car?

Comparatives You form the comparative of one-syllable adjectives by adding *-er*. For adjectives ending in *-e*, you add *-r*. For adjectives that end in one vowel and one consonant, you double the last letter.
You're much taller and nicer than your brother.
London is bigger than Paris.

⚠️ Don't use *more* with the comparative of one-syllable adjectives.
The country is quieter than the city.
NOT *The country is more quieter than the city.*

You form the comparative of two-syllable and longer adjectives with *more* + adjective. For two-syllable adjectives ending in *y*, you change the *y* to *i* and add *-er*.
Rugby is more exciting than football.
The first exam was easier than the second.

Too and **very** Don't confuse *too* with *very*. *Too* can mean 'more than enough' or 'more than necessary'. You can use *very* to make adjectives or adverbs stronger.
This curry is too spicy for me. (I can't eat it.)
This curry is very spicy. (It's more spicy than usual but I can eat it.)

You can use *too* + adjective or adverb and an infinitive structure.
It's too hot to go for a walk.

Such You use *such ... that* to give an explanation for something. Never use *a such*, use *such a* or leave out *such ... that* and change the structure of the sentence.
It was such an interesting film that I saw it twice. NOT *It was a such interesting film that I saw it twice.*
It was an interesting film, so I saw it twice.

Articles You don't use an article with meals, days, months, holidays, special days or festivals.
What time shall we have lunch?
I'll see you on Friday.
I was born in May.
What do you do at Easter?
We're having a party on New Year's Day.

Test it ✔

1 **Circle the correct option.**

She's always late! It's just so ~~disconsiderate~~/(inconsiderate.)

a You behave in a very unresponsible/irresponsible way.
b Funnily/Funnyly enough, I was just thinking about you when you called.
c Everywhere she looked, she saw unorder/disorder and chaos!
d My grandmother thinks my life's incomplete/uncomplete because I'm single.
e Congratulations! Here's the confirmation/confirment of your job offer.
f Stealing is unlegal/illegal and not very nice!
g The more I eat, the fater/fatter I get.
h There was a cancellation/cancel so we got an appointment.
i David completely unagrees/disagrees on this point.
j Nicky didn't mean to do it. It was accidental/accidentist.

2 **Look at the words in bold and correct any mistakes.**

Since going on a diet, I've been feeling a lot **fiter**.   *fitter*

a Tina belongs to the Society for Scientific **Exploration**.   ....
b This is the **noisyest** street in Berlin.   ....
c Dad's handwriting is **illegible**. I can't read it at all.   ....
d Today was the **hottest** day of the year.   ....
e I feel **incompetent** because I can't understand this report.   ....
f And they all lived **happily** ever after.   ....
g Do you think Sandra is being **unrespectful**?   ....
h Many verbs in English are **irregular**.   ....
i This **organizement** is very good.   ....
j I don't like John because he's very **criticing**.   ....

20

GO to page 24 and check your answers.

Test it again ✔

Read the text below. Use the word given in capitals at the end of each line to form a word that fits in the space in the same line.

KEEPING KIDS AT SCHOOL

People are (1) .... of parents who can't control their children, but	CRITIC
according to statistics, (2) .... among teenagers is increasing.	OBEY
It is (3) .... for children to miss school, but many do play truant.	LEGAL
Experts say that the younger the parents, the (4) .... the danger	BIG
that their (5) .... as adults will affect their children's schooling.	EXPERIENCE
Children must be encouraged not to think of school as an (6)	RELEVANT
part of life. This will create a (7) .... from positive to negative	TRANSFORM
feelings. We must remember that only a few children (8) .... from	APPEAR
school each year and schools now offer many (9) .... activities.	ADDITION
The days of children (10) .... enjoying education are not over yet!	HAPPY

1 CRITIC	....	6 RELEVANT ....
2 OBEY	....	7 TRANSFORM ....
3 LEGAL	....	8 APPEAR ....
4 BIG	....	9 ADDITION ....
5 EXPERIENCE		10 HAPPY ....

20

Fix it

Answers to Test it

Check your answers. Wrong answer?
Read the right Fix it note to find out why.

1 • inconsiderate → C
- **a** irresponsible → D
- **b** Funnily → A
- **c** disorder → B
- **d** incomplete → C
- **e** confirmation → E
- **f** illegal → D
- **g** fatter → A
- **h** cancellation → E
- **i** disagrees → B
- **j** accidental → F

2 • fitter → A
- **a** correct → E
- **b** noisiest → A
- **c** correct → D
- **d** correct → A
- **e** correct → C
- **f** correct → A
- **g** disrespectful → B
- **h** correct → D
- **i** organization → E
- **j** critical → F

Now go to page 23. Test yourself again.

Answers to Test it again

1 critical
2 disobedience
3 illegal
4 bigger
5 inexperience
6 irrelevant
7 transformation
8 disappear
9 additional
10 happily

Fix it notes

A Be careful with the spelling of words that you make from other words. For adjectives ending in -y, change the y to an i. For adjectives ending in a short vowel + consonant, double the consonant.

B To make the opposite of some adjectives, nouns and verbs, add dis- e.g. disobedient, disobedience, disobey. Note that more than one change to the root word is sometimes necessary.

C To make the opposite of some adjectives, add in-, e.g. incomplete, incompetent.

D To make the opposite of adjectives beginning with l-, add il-. For adjectives beginning with r-, add ir-, e.g. illegal, irreversible.

E To make nouns from some verbs, add -ation, e.g. confirm → confirmation.

F To make an adjective from some nouns, add -al, e.g. critic → critical.

For more information, see the Review page opposite. ▷

i Review

Word-building You can form new parts of speech (nouns, adverbs, adjectives, etc.) from other parts of speech, often by adding a prefix or a suffix. A prefix goes before the word and a suffix goes after the word. For example, with the adjective *happy* you can add the prefix *un-* to form its opposite adjective, *unhappy*. You can also add the suffix *-ness* to form a noun, *happiness*.

Nouns and adverbs from adjectives Be careful with the spelling of words that you make from other words. For adjectives ending in *-y*, change the *-y* to an *-i*. For adjectives ending in a short vowel + consonant, you need to double the consonant.
Happiness is what most people want.
Happily, everyone survived the crash.

Opposites of adjectives To make the opposite of some adjectives, nouns and verbs, you add the prefix *dis-* e.g. *disobedient, distasteful, disrespect*. Note that more than one change to the root word is sometimes necessary.
obedient ➜ *disobedience*
respect ➜ *disrespect*

You make the opposite of some adjectives by adding the prefix *in-*, e.g. *incomplete, incompetent*.
The witness's story was inaccurate and incomplete.

You make the opposite of some adjectives beginning with *l-* by adding the prefix *il-*, e.g. *illegal*. For some adjectives beginning with *r-*, you add the prefix *ir-*, e.g. *irreversible*.
Everything I like is illegal, immoral or fattening.

Adjectives from nouns You can make an adjective from some nouns by adding the suffix *-al*, e.g. *critic* ➜ *critical*.
The musical we saw on Broadway was magical. The kids loved it.
Joey is incredibly critical of everything, isn't he?

Nouns from verbs You can make nouns from some verbs by adding the suffix *-ation*, e.g. *explore* ➜ *exploration*. Again, you may or may not need to make spelling changes.
confirm: We will send confirmation to you by email.
explore: The exploration of the lunar crater will happen later this month.
clarify: Could you please give us all a little clarification?

Multiple-choice cloze (2)

Test it ✔

1 **Choose the correct phrasal verbs to complete the sentences.**

burst out   listen out   fill in   break down   drop out   make out

I'm worried the van will ....*break down*........ before we get to Romania.
a Please remember to .... for further announcements about flight BA082.
b I'm convinced Nick is going to .... of university.
c Amanda took one look at me and .... laughing.
d Can you speak up? I can't .... what you're saying.
e Kindly .... the form and take it to the office on the third floor.

2 **Circle the best option.**

You were always on my mind/heart/brain/soul.
a You need to improve your attitude/opinion/view/aspect.
b It's a very good possibility/event/opportunity/occasion to make a real difference to children's lives.
c We saw the advice/news/advertisement/publicity for your flat in the paper.
d This is an old English custom/behaviour/habit/manner.
e Did you hear the news/publicity/advice/advertisement about the prime minister's divorce?
f If/Unless/When/Although it rains, we'll have a picnic.
g The population hasn't grown much this decade. There are actually/currently/immediately/nowadays about a million people in the city.
h The Citroen C4 VTR is very common/popular/ordinary/average this year.
i What I like most is Joe's sense of personality/character/mood/humour.
j I haven't got a pet. Actually/Currently/Presently/Immediately I'm allergic to cat and dog fur.

3 **Complete the sentences with a suitable preposition.**

We got there in the end, thanks ...*to*... you.
a That's very good advice. I'll keep it .... mind.
b What do you do .... a living?
c Thanks .... all your hard work on the project.
d Kevin had a change .... heart and decide to take the job after all.
e I do wish you'd make .... your mind.

20

GO to page 28 and check your answers.

Test it again ✔

Read the text below and decide which answer (A, B, C or D) best fits each space.

MY FIRST JOB

When I was 19, I (1) .... out of my university course and ended up getting a job in a local travel agent's. I'd seen the (2) .... for the job in the local paper. It said they wanted someone with a nice (3) .... and a friendly (4) .... I thought the job might be an (5) .... to send people to interesting places and to see some of the world myself. (6) ...., it turned out to be a bit of joke. I arrived at work on the first day with a positive (7) ...., ready to work and learn about new places. I spent that morning and every morning for the first three months filling (8) .... forms and making coffee for the rest of the staff. (9) .... I was hoping to be dealing with travel-hungry people with a good idea of where they wanted to go, the (10) .... customer took ages to make their mind (11) .... It was amazing the number of customers who would spend ages finding the perfect destination only to have a change (12) .... heart at the last moment. If we did organize the trip of a lifetime for someone, we rarely got thanks (13) .... all our efforts. I now work in publishing (14) .... a living, so these days I'm a customer in travel agencies. One thing I always keep (15) .... mind is the need to say thank you.

1	A dropped	B made	C listened	D burst
2	A publicity	B news	C advertisement	D advice
3	A mood	B character	C humour	D personality
4	A manner	B custom	C behaviour	D habit
5	A occasion	B opportunity	C possibility	D chance
6	A Presently	B Currently	C Actually	D Nowadays
7	A view	B attitude	C opinion	D aspect
8	A in	B up	C down	D through
9	A If	B When	C Unless	D Although
10	A popular	B ordinary	C average	D common
11	A through	B in	C down	D up
12	A in	B of	C to	D with
13	A of	B with	C by	D for
14	A from	B for	C to	D with
15	A to	B under	C in	D of

15

Fix it

Answers to Test it

Check your answers. Wrong answer?
Read the right Fix it note to find out why.

1 • break down → A
a listen out → A
b drop out → A
c burst out → A
d make out → A
e fill out → A

2 • mind → A
a attitude → C
b opportunity → C
c advertisement → D
d custom → E
e news → D
f Unless → F
g currently → F
h popular → G
i humour → B
j actually → F

3 • to → A
a in → A
b for → A
c for → A
d of → A
e up → A

> Now go to page 27. Test yourself again.

Answers to Test it again

1 A	9 D
2 C	10 C
3 D	11 D
4 A	12 B
5 B	13 D
6 C	14 B
7 B	15 C
8 A	

Fix it notes

A Phrasal verbs often have different meanings from the base verb. Many fixed expressions and phrases contain a preposition.

B Words often have similar meanings but they go with certain other words and phrases, e.g. *sense of humour*.

C A *possibility* or a *chance* is something that may (not) happen; an *opportunity* is a good time for doing something. An *attitude* is a way of behaving; an *opinion* is a way of thinking.

D *Advice* is an opinion about what you should (not) do. *An advertisement* tries to make people buy something. *Publicity* is making something well known. *News* is information about a recent event.

E *Customs* are the traditions of a society. *Habits* are things you do regularly (often without thinking). Your *manner* is the way you behave and talk to people.

F *Currently* means 'at the moment'. Use *actually* to give new information about what you've just said. Use *although* to make a contrast. Use *unless* to mean 'if not'.

G *Popular* means that people like something. *Common* means that there's a lot of a particular thing. *Average* means 'typical' or 'usual'. *Ordinary* means 'not different' or 'special'.

> For more information, see the Review page opposite.

ⓘ Review

- In part 1 of paper 3 look at the options, A–D, carefully. Cross out any that you are sure are wrong.
- Make sure your answer fits both the meaning and the grammar of the sentence.
- Be careful with phrasal verbs – make sure your answer fits the context.

See page 86 for a description of this part of the Use of English paper.

Phrasal verbs The short words that follow the base verb of a phrasal verb can often change the meaning, e.g. *make out* is not the same as *make up*. Try to make a note of the different verbs and learn their meanings as you go along.
It was dark. I couldn't make out who was there.   She made up a silly story.

Fixed expressions Many fixed expressions and phrases contain a preposition, e.g. *change of heart*.
He had a change of heart and decided not to go.

Words often have similar meanings but they go with certain other words and phrases, e.g. *be in a good mood*.
Why is he in such a good mood?

Possibilities and opportunities A *possibility* or a *chance* is something that may or may not happen. An *opportunity* is a good time for doing something.
Is there a possibility of a strike?
There's no chance of getting a table – they're fully booked.
This is a great opportunity for us to make new friends.

Attitudes and opinions An *attitude* is a way of behaving; you *have an attitude to/towards* someone or something. An *opinion* is a way of thinking; you *have an opinion on/about* a subject and *of* a person. *Advice* is an opinion about what you should or shouldn't do.
We have different opinions about life.
Tom's so mean – he has such a bad attitude towards money.
Thanks for the advice on where to go.

Advertising and news An *advertisement* tries to make people buy something and can appear on TV, on the radio, in the press, etc. *Publicity* is the business of making something or someone well known. *News* is information about a recent event.
TV advertisements are often funny.
She's getting a lot of publicity for her film.
There was some bad news about taxes.

Customs and habits *Customs* are the traditions of a society or group. *Habits* are the good and bad things you do regularly (often without thinking). Your *manner* is the way you behave and talk.
I tried to respect Greek customs when I lived in Athens.
Chewing your nails is a horrible habit.
She has a very friendly manner.

Popular means that a lot of people like something. *Common* means that there's a lot of a particular thing. *Average* means typical or usual. *Ordinary* means not different or special.
Peru is popular for holidays this year.
Deer are very common in this area.
The average person works seven hours a day.
The meal was expensive, but the food was ordinary.

Currently and actually *Currently* means 'at the moment'.
He's currently working in Poland.

⚠ Don't use *actually* to mean 'at the moment'. Use *actually* to give new information about what you've just said.
I've known Emma for years. Actually, she's one of my oldest friends.

Although and unless Use *although* to make a contrast. *Unless* means 'if not'.
I'm feeling better, although I'm still tired.
I'll see you tonight unless I have to work late.

Open cloze (2)

Test it ✔

1 **Choose the correct words to complete the sentences.**

any   in   but   could   been   for   that   are   it   at   ~~of~~

Who's Afraid ...*of*.... *Virginia Woolf* is a play by Edward Albee.
a   People still listen to sixties' music but it was better .... the eighties!
b   Harry says these computers .... made in Taiwan.
c   I'm not going to buy this house. I'd never be able to sell .... again.
d   Tina's never .... abroad. She's scared of flying.
e   Are you going to go .... that job you told me about?
f   Last week it was so hot that we .... not even go outside.
g   Oliver, you're one of the luckiest people .... I know!
h   Vanessa says one thing .... she does the opposite.
i   Eric and Anne were living in Istanbul .... the time.
j   You won't have .... trouble passing the test. It's easy.

2 **Circle the correct option.**

He resigned (so)/that he could spend more time with his family.
a   Don't forget to take some ID so that they are going to let/let you in.
b   Great news! All my problems solved/were solved last night.
c   Do you think there are some/any biscuits left? We ate a lot yesterday.
d   David came to see me, so I took him/David out to lunch.
e   Both my kids are afraid for/of the dark.
f   Fiji is the place where/which Lisse grew up.
g   The forecast said it would be rainy but/in spite it's sunny.
h   We'll leave to/at one o'clock and get there by seven.
i   What would you like to do tonight? It's up for/to you.
j   Have you ever been/Did you ever go to Tokyo before?

| 20 |

GO to page 32 and check your answers.

Test it again ✔

**Read the text below and think of the word which best fits each space.
Use only one word in each space.**

WHAT CAR? WHAT COLOUR?

Be careful about the colour of car (1) .... you buy. Experts
(2) .... said that the value of a second-hand car can vary
(3) .... up to 10% just because of its colour. It seems that today
nobody wants white cars. In fact, white is (4) .... unpopular that
it (5) .... reduce the value of the car by thousands of euros
when the owner decides to sell (6) .... So what's a safe colour
to choose? Well, if you go (7) .... silver, you won't have
(8) .... problems in re-selling.

But why is colour important? 'It is mainly down (9) .... fashion,'
says a car expert. '(10) .... the 1980s and 1990s, red and white
were very popular. Now, they (11) .... seen as old-fashioned
and silver is the best alternative. It looks good on most models of car and
buyers want to follow the trend so that they don't lose money.'

Colour has always (12) .... a factor in making cars.
Henry Ford made the Model T only in black – not because it looked better,
(13) .... because it was the cheapest colour to paint a car
(14) .... that time. Even as late as the mid-1950s one-third of all
cars that (15) .... sold in Britain were black.

15

🔧 Fix it

Answers to Test it

Check your answers. Wrong answer?
Read the right Fix it note to find out why.

1 • of → E
  a in → G
  b are → B
  c it → D
  d been → B
  e for → E
  f couldn't → C
  g that → A
  h but → C
  i at → G
  j any → F

2 • so → C
  a let → C
  b were solved → B
  c any → F
  d him → D
  e of → E
  f where → A
  g but → C
  h at → G
  i to → E
  j Have you ever been → B

Now go to page 31. Test yourself again.

Answers to Test it again

1 that
2 have
3 by
4 so
5 can/could/will/may/might
6 it
7 for
8 any/many
9 to
10 In/During
11 are
12 been
13 but
14 at
15 were

🔧 Fix it notes

A This sentence includes a defining relative clause. Begin these clauses with *who* or *that* for people, *that* or *which* for objects, *where* for a place.

B Form the present perfect with *has/have* + past participle. Form the passive with an appropriate tense of *be* + past participle.

C Usually use *so* (*that*) + a modal verb (*can*, *will*, etc.) or the present simple to give the purpose for an action. You can also use *so* before an adjective or adverb to say why something happens. Use *but* to express a contrast or difference between two things.

D Use object pronouns (*him*, *her*, *it*, etc.) to avoid repeating a noun in a sentence.

E Be aware of words that go together. These are often phrasal verbs, e.g. *go for*, or verb/adjective + preposition, e.g. *wait for*, *afraid of*.

F Use *any* in negative sentences and in most questions with uncountable and plural nouns when you're talking about a small amount or number.

G Use *in* with long periods of time, e.g. *in the 1970s*. Use *at* with a fixed point in time and clock times, e.g. *at that point in my life*, *at nine o'clock*.

For more information, see the Review page opposite. ▷

ⓘ Review

EXAM TIP

- In part 2 of paper 3 fill in the gaps that you're sure about first. It's easier to go back and complete the task when most of the answers are in place.
- Write only one word for each gap when you transfer your answers to the answer sheet.

See page 86 for a description of this part of the Use of English paper.

Relative clauses Some sentences contain relative clauses. A relative clause adds information to the main part of the sentence and often starts with a relative pronoun (*who, that, which, where,* etc.). You use *who* or *that* to talk about people, *that* or *which* to talk about objects, and *where* to talk about places.
Jo's the girl who I met last week.
Where's the CD that I bought yesterday?
This is the house where my father was born.

⚠ Don't leave out the relative pronoun in non-defining relative clauses.
Richard, who lives near me, has just won the lottery. NOT *Richard, lives near me, has just won the lottery.*

Present perfect You form the present perfect with *has/have* + past participle. Remember that some past participles are irregular. Learn these as you go along.
I've never flown in a balloon.

The passive You form the passive with an appropriate tense of *be* + past participle. Remember that the object of an active sentence becomes the subject of a passive sentence.
They will deliver the boxes in June.
→ *The boxes will be delivered in June.*

So (that) You usually use *so (that)* + a modal verb (*can, will,* etc.) or the present simple to give the purpose for an action.
Take a torch so that you can see where you are going.

You can also use *so* + adjective/adverb *that* ... to say why something happens.
The wind was so strong that the trees were blown down.
He drove so slowly that we were late.

But You use *but* to express a contrast or difference between two things.
I'd like to buy a new car, but I can't afford one.

Object pronouns You use object pronouns (*him, her, it,* etc.) to avoid repeating a noun in the same sentence or in sentences that follow.
My sister is visiting from the States.
Would you like to meet her?

Collocations Be aware of prepositions in collocations (words that go together). These are often phrasal verbs, e.g. *go for, work out.* They can also be verb/adjective + preposition, e.g. *wait for, afraid of.*
Have you made up your mind yet?
I couldn't work out the answer.
Don't wait for me – I'm going to be late.
Are you afraid of spiders?

Any You use *any* in negative sentences and in most questions with uncountable and plural nouns when you're talking about a small amount or number.
We haven't got any petrol.
Is there any rice left?
Have you got any job vacancies at the moment?

Prepositions of time You use *in* with long periods of time, e.g. *in the 1970s.* You use *at* with a fixed point in time and clock times, e.g. *at that time, at 9.00.*
My grandmother was born in the 1950s.
At that point in my life, we were living in Paris.
Let's meet at midday.

Test it ✔

1 Choose the correct words to complete the sentences. There are four words you don't need.

as   as if   because   because of   either   get   to go   got
like   ~~to look~~   making   the problem   to see   taking   with

The teacher didn't have time ......*to look*.............. at the students' homework.

a Sean is interested in .... a course in Spanish conversation.

b Let's take a map in case we .... lost.

c Wake up! It's time .... to school!

d English grammar is .... algebra – difficult to learn and sometimes hard to understand.

e The road was blocked .... the accident.

f I'd really like .... you again so let's try to meet in September.

g We could .... go camping or stay in a bed and breakfast.

h The kids built a sandcastle. They used a piece of paper ....
a flag.

i Jodie got a dog .... she was lonely.

j Why don't you calm down and explain .... to me?

2 Find and correct six mistakes in the sentences.

The train was late. It was a silly decision ~~catching~~ it.   ..*to catch*...

a Mike can't stand to watch sports.   ....

b Neither my brother nor my sister is married.   ....

c I couldn't sleep last night because jet-lag.   ....

d Amanda suggested me the idea.   ....

e Patrick works like a civil servant in a government department.   ....

f Take some aspirins with you in case you'll get a headache.   ....

g I wish to speak to the manager, please.   ....

h Unfortunately, he's terrible at to do maths.   ....

i One day she hopes to be a landscape gardener.   ....

j Sometimes, being in love is like having an illness.   ....

20

GO to page 36 and check your answers.

Test it again ✔

Complete the second sentence so that it has a similar meaning to the first sentence, using the word given. Do not change the word given. You must use between two and five words, including the word given.

1   Paul gave us a description of the castle.
    described
    Paul ....

2   The rain stopped the tennis match.
    because
    The tennis match was stopped ....

3   It was good to see David last Monday.
    enjoyed
    I .... David last Monday.

4   Joe didn't go to school. Nor did Keith.
    neither
    .... went to school.

5   Mr Larkin was a librarian at the university.
    as
    Mr Larkin .... at the university.

6   My best friend plays the violin well.
    good
    My best friend .... the violin.

7   It may be hot so take some sunscreen.
    case
    Take some sunscreen ....

8   What Jo really hates is driving at night.
    stand
    Jo really .... at night.

9   They showed us the route in detail.
    to
    They .... in detail.

10 My cousin decided to take a year off.
    decision
    My cousin made .... a year off.

20

🔧 Fix it

Answers to Test it

Check your answers. Wrong answer?
Read the right Fix it note to find out why.

1
•	to look	→	C
a	taking	→	B
b	get	→	D
c	to go	→	C
d	like	→	F
e	because of	→	D
f	to see	→	A
e	either	→	E
e	as	→	F
e	because	→	D
e	the problem	→	G

2
•	~~getting~~ to get	→	C
a	~~to watch~~ watching	→	A
b	correct	→	E
c	~~because~~ because of	→	D
d	~~me the idea~~ the idea to me	→	G
e	~~like~~ as	→	F
f	~~you'll get~~ you get	→	D
g	correct	→	A
h	~~to do~~ doing	→	B
i	correct	→	A
j	correct	→	F

Now go to page 35. Test yourself again.

Answers to Test it again

(2 marks for each correct sentence)
1. described the castle to us
2. because of the rain/because it was raining
3. enjoyed seeing
4. Neither Joe nor Keith
5. worked as a librarian
6. is good at (playing)
7. in case it's hot
8. can't stand driving
9. showed the route to us
10. a decision to take

🔧 Fix it notes

A Use an *-ing* form after some verbs, e.g. *love, like, enjoy, can't stand,* and an infinitive after others, e.g. *want, wish, hope, teach, decide, would like.*

B You often use an infinitive after an adjective, e.g. *good to see you.* Use an *-ing* form after an adjective + preposition, e.g. *good at cooking.*

C After some nouns (e.g. *decision, time, need*), use an infinitive, not the base form or *-ing* form.

D Use *because* before a subject + verb. Use *because of* before a pronoun or noun. Use *in case* to talk about future possibilities. Be careful! Always use the present simple after *in case.*

E Use *either ... or* to talk about two parallel or similar possibilities. Use *neither ... nor* for two parallel or similar negative actions or situations.

F Use *like* (often before a noun or pronoun) to say that one thing is similar to another. Use *as* to talk about someone's job or to say what something is used for.

G Put indirect objects after direct objects with the verbs *describe, explain, say* and *suggest.*

> For more information, see the Review page opposite. ▷

ⓘ Review

EXAM TIP

- In part 3 of paper 3 look at the words around the gap and identify what structure you need to use.
- Decide what part of the first sentence needs to be used in the gap in the second sentence.

See page 86 for a description of this part of the Use of English paper.

Verb patterns You use an *-ing* form after some verbs, e.g. *love, like, enjoy, can't stand*, and an infinitive after others, e.g. *want, wish, hope, teach, decide, would like*. Make a note of these patterns and try to learn them as you go along.
I can't stand waiting in queues.
She hopes to be a professional musician.

Adjective + verb You often use an infinitive after an adjective, e.g. *good to see you*. You use an *-ing* form after an adjective + preposition, e.g. *good at cooking*.
It's great to hear from you.
I'm tired of working.

Noun + verb After some nouns (e.g. *decision, time, need*), you use an infinitive, not the base form or *-ing* form.
It's time to go now.   NOT   ~~It's time go now.~~   OR   ~~It's time going now.~~

Because (of) and *in case* You use *because* before a subject + verb. You use *because of* before a pronoun or noun. You use *in case* to talk about future possibilities.
Jake was late because he overslept.
The match was postponed because of the rain.
Here's my number in case you need to call me.

⚠ You always use the present simple to refer to the future after *in case*.
Here's some money in case you need it.
NOT   ~~Here's some money in case you will need it.~~

Either ... or and *neither ... nor* You use *either ... or* to talk about two parallel or similar possibilities. You use *neither ... nor* for two parallel or similar negative actions or situations. You don't use negative verb forms with *neither ... nor*.
You can have either pasta or pizza.
Neither my sister nor my brother can drive.

Like and *as* You use *like* (often before a noun or pronoun) to say that one thing is similar to another. You use *as* to talk about someone's job or to say what something is used for.
I'm just like my mother.
Joe is a teacher, like me.
Sam works as a dentist.
You can use this pen as a torch.

Direct and indirect objects You put indirect objects after direct objects with the verbs *describe, explain, say* and *suggest*.
Oliver described his new job to us.
NOT   ~~Oliver described us his new job.~~
Amy explained the problem to her teacher.   NOT   ~~Amy explained her teacher the problem.~~
You suggested this route to me.
NOT   ~~You suggested me this route.~~

Error correction (2)

Test it ✔

1 True or false?

			TRUE	FALSE
	A	Don't hurry yourself so much, there's plenty of time.		
	B	It took me a long time to learn how to relax myself.		
		Neither of these sentences is correct.	☑	☐
a	**A**	Bridgid looks very much happier since she got her new job.		
	B	You look very much happy today, David!		
		Both of these sentences are correct.	☐	☐
b	**A**	My darling boy, you've made me be a very happy person.		
	B	I adore him because he lets me do what I want.		
		Only one of these sentences is possible.	☐	☐
c	**A**	Vicky's slowly getting over the break-up of her relationship.		
	B	Don't interrupt me! I'm getting irritated.		
		One of these sentences contains a phrasal verb.	☐	☐
d	**A**	Some of us like red wine and others don't.		
	B	Some my friends don't like wine at all.		
		Neither of these sentences is possible.	☐	☐
e	**A**	Eileen's great – she's so interesting to talk to.		
	B	Of all games, snooker is the most boring to watch it.		
		Both of these sentences are incorrect.	☐	☐

2 Cross out the extra word in the six incorrect sentences.

Mum always lets me ~~to~~ watch cartoons after school.

a Except for a few rainy days, it's been an exceptionally good summer.
b What Sylvia really needs is an office to work in it.
c I've never laughed at any of your jokes.
d Please concentrate yourself on the problem.
e I'm so sorry I made you to cry.
f Please give up a detailed account of what happened.
g He takes everyone seriously except me.
h Have I ever told you how much you make me smile?
i Some of the news on TV last night was terribly sad.
j She was very much sorry that she didn't see you.
k We gave the dog a bone to chew it.

	16

GO to page 40 and check your answers.

Test it again ✔

Read the text below and look carefully at each line. Some of the lines are correct, and some have a word which should not be there. If a line is correct, put a tick (✓) next to it. If a line has a word that should not be there, cross it out.

BIG DECISIONS

1 Isn't it strange the way some people seem to know what they want to do with
2 their lives, even when they're quite young? Some of people I was at university
3 with knew that they were going to be accountants or start out a new business.
4 I had no idea. I did up a course in modern languages but I knew I didn't want
5 to teach French or Italian. I don't like making children to learn things. I prefer
6 it when people learn because they really want to. I studied very much
7 hard at university but that was mostly because I couldn't relax myself. I liked
8 some of the literature we studied, particularly the sixteenth-century poetry. My
9 professor, Malcolm Smith, gave me some books to read them. One was a travel
10 diary by the French philosopher, Montaigne. After that, I read everything I could
11 find. In fact, I don't think I stopped reading except for when I had to take my final
12 exams. I just loved it. Looking back, I realize that I was very much more serious
13 as a student in my final year than I'd been in the previous two years. I discovered
14 that the sixteenth century was an interesting period to research it. I suppose that's
15 why I felt myself more at ease and eventually became a university professor.

15

🔧 Fix it

Answers to Test it

Check your answers. Wrong answer?
Read the right Fix it note to find out why.

1
- True → A
- a False → G
- b True → B
- c True → D
- d False → F
- e False → C

2
- to → B
- a correct → E
- b it → C
- c correct → F
- d yourself → A
- e to → B
- f up → D
- g correct → E
- h correct → B
- i correct → F
- j much → G
- k it → C

Now go to page 39. Test yourself again.

Answers to Test it again

1 ✔
2 ~~of~~
3 ~~out~~
4 ~~up~~
5 ~~to~~
6 ~~much~~
7 ~~myself~~
8 ✔
9 ~~them~~
10 ✔
11 ~~for~~
12 ✔
13 ✔
14 ~~it~~
15 ~~myself~~

🔧 Fix it notes

A Don't use reflexive pronouns (*myself, ourselves*) with the verbs *relax, concentrate, feel* and *hurry*.

B Use the base form, not the infinitive, after *make* + object and *let* + object. After *make* + object + adjective or noun, you don't use the verb *be* before the adjective or noun.

C In adjective + infinitive structures, you don't use an object pronoun after *the*. In noun + infinitive structures, you don't use an object pronoun after the infinitive.

D Look carefully at the verbs in a sentence. Check to see if they're phrasal verbs or not.

E Use *except*, not *except for*, before a preposition or a conjunction.

F Use *some of* and *any of*, not *some* and *any*, before words like *the, my, this*.

G Use *very*, not *very much*, before adjectives and adverbs. You can use *very much* with a comparative adjective or adverb.

> For more information, see the Review page opposite. ▷

ℹ Review

EXAM TIP

- In part 4 of paper 3 don't forget to focus on the first word on each line and last word on each line in case it is the extra word.
- Don't confuse extra words that are mistakes with words that just add extra information to the sentence, e.g. *really*, *very*, etc.

See page 86 for a description of this part of the Use of English paper.

Reflexive pronouns Be careful with reflexive verbs. If a verb is reflexive in your language, it may not be reflexive in English.

⚠ You don't use reflexive pronouns (*myself, ourselves*, etc.) with the verbs *relax, concentrate, feel* and *hurry*.
Just relax after your journey. NOT ~~Just relax yourself after your journey.~~
We can't concentrate with all this noise. NOT ~~We can't concentrate ourselves with all this noise.~~
Why do you feel sad? NOT ~~Why do you feel yourself sad?~~
They had to hurry to catch the train. NOT ~~They had to hurry themselves to catch the train.~~

Make and *let* You use the base form (not the infinitive) after *make* + object and *let* + object.
The teacher made us stay behind after school.
Will you let me use your car?

After *make* + object + adjective or noun, you don't use the verb *be* before the adjective or noun.
The heat made me tired. NOT ~~The heat made me be tired.~~

Object pronouns In adjective + infinitive structures, you don't use an object pronoun after the infinitive. In noun + infinitive structures, you don't use an object pronoun after the infinitive.
Annie is really easy to work with. NOT ~~Annie is really easy to work with her.~~
They gave the children a DVD to watch. NOT ~~They gave the children a DVD to watch it.~~

Phrasal verbs Phrasal verbs are verbs followed by a short word, e.g. *down, across, through*. In part 4 of the Use of English paper, these short words may be the extra words that you need to find. Look carefully at the verbs in a sentence to check whether they're phrasal verbs.

Except You use *except*, not *except for*, before a preposition or a conjunction. You can use *except for* before a noun.
It was a good concert except that it was rather short.
We had a great holiday except for the weather.

Some of and *any of* You use *some of* and *any of*, not *some* and *any*, before words like *the, my, this*.
Some of the staff went on strike. NOT ~~Some the staff went on strike.~~
I would lend my flat to any of my friends. NOT ~~I would lend my flat to any my friends.~~

Very and *very much* You use *very*, not *very much*, before adjectives and adverbs. You can use *very much* with a comparative adjective or adverb.
Your laptop is very fast. NOT ~~Your laptop is very much fast.~~
The band played very loudly. NOT ~~The band played very much loudly.~~
It's very much colder today.
I feel very much better.

Word formation (2)

Test it ✔

1 **Complete the sentences. Use the correct form of the words in brackets.**

It's the middle of November and the sun is ......*shining*............... (shine).

a   There has been a great .... (improve) in sales in recent months.

b   My brother wants to work as a .... (biology).

c   High heels are very .... (practical) shoes for a hiking holiday.

d   Do robots have the .... (able) to think?

e   I got the .... (impress) that something was wrong.

f   Nobody else objects to the plan. What are your .... (object)?

g   I think .... (walk) is the best form of exercise.

h   Please reply to this message .... (immediate).

i   You don't like going to the gym? Why not get a personal ....
    (train)?

j   You need a good .... (imagine) to be a poet.

2 **Circle the correct option, A or B.**

After five years, Jim was promoted to ....
(A) manager   B managist

a   The arrival of the film stars caused a lot of ....
    A exciting   B excitement

b   The children ran .... down the street.
    A noisily   B noisy

c   You will have .... for the new sales campaign.
    A responsibility   B responsible

d   Please don't be so ....
    A inpatient   B impatient

e   Thank you for your ....
    A co-operation   B co-operating

f   Why would you like to be a .... ?
    A psychologer   B psychologist

| 16 |

GO to page 44 and check your answers.

Test it again ✔

Read the text below. Use the word given in capitals at the end of each line to form a word that fits in the space in the same line.

THE CHANGING WORLD OF WORK

Some people stop work and look forward to a long (1) .... , but **RETIRE**
a (2) .... in the field of ageing has said that opinions are changing. **SOCIOLOGY**
Many older people don't want to stop work (3) .... and take up **COMPLETE**
a life of (4) .... . Instead, they hope to continue in some sort of paid **RELAX**
(5) .... , but to work less intensively. There will also be much more **EMPLOY**
(6) .... in the work people do. Instead of doing the same job for life, **DIVERSE**
older (7) .... will have several jobs, which is known as 'portfolio **WORK**
working'. It is (8) .... to know how all this will affect the world of work, **POSSIBLE**
but it's clear that there will be more (9) .... for jobs. People will also **COMPETE**
need to develop their skills and take up (10) .... at any time in their life. **TRAIN**

1 RETIRE ....

2 SOCIOLOGY ....

3 COMPLETE ....

4 RELAX ....

5 EMPLOY ....

6 DIVERSE ....

7 WORK ....

8 POSSIBLE ....

9 COMPETE ....

10 TRAIN ....

10

🔧 Fix it

Answers to Test it

Check your answers. Wrong answer?
Read the right Fix it note to find out why.

1 • shining → D
   a improvement → A
   b biologist → C
   c impractical → G
   d ability → E
   e impression → A
   f objection → A
   g walking → D
   h immediately → F
   i trainer → B
   j imagination → A

2 • A → B
   a B → A
   b A → F
   c A → E
   d B → G
   e A → A
   f B → C

◀ Now go to page 43. Test yourself again.

Answers to Test it again

1 retirement
2 sociologist
3 completely
4 relaxation
5 employment
6 diversity
7 workers
8 impossible
9 competition
10 training

🔧 Fix it notes

A To make a noun from some verbs, add: -ment, e.g. entertain → entertainment; -ion, e.g. object → objection. You sometimes need to change or add to the base verb, e.g. imagine → imagination.

B To make a personal noun from some verbs, add: -r or -er, e.g. paint → painter.

C To make a personal noun from some other nouns, use -ist, e.g. economics → economist. You always need to make changes to the spelling of the noun.

D To make the gerund (noun form) from some verbs, add -ing, e.g. go → going. You sometimes need to make changes to the base verb, e.g. shine → shining.

E To make a noun from some adjectives, use -ity, e.g. able → ability. You usually need to make some changes to the spelling of the noun.

F To make adverbs from most adjectives, add -ly, e.g. quick → quickly. You sometimes need to make changes to the spelling of the adjective, e.g. noisy → noisily.

G To make some adjectives beginning with m- or p- negative, add im-, e.g. practical → impractical.

> For more information, see the Review page opposite. ▷

ⓘ Review

EXAM TIP

- In part 5 of paper 3 look for clues that you need a plural noun, e.g. plural verb forms, words like *several*, *a lot of*, etc.
- Don't just write the first word that you know that can be formed from the base word – make sure the new word fits the context.

See page 86 for a description of this part of the Use of English paper.

Suffix -ly You can form adverbs from most regular adjectives by adding the suffix -ly. You may need to make some spelling changes. For example, -y changes to -i and then you add -ly.
happy → happily
quick → quickly
soft → softly

⚠ You can't form adverbs from all adjectives. With some, you need to use a phrase instead. For example, *friendly* becomes *in a friendly way*.

Prefix im- You can make the opposite of some adjectives that begin with an *m-* or a *p-* by using the prefix *im-*. Here are some common examples.
practical → impractical
possible → impossible
patient → impatient
mature → immature
moral → immoral

Suffix -ity You can form a noun from some adjectives by using the suffix -ity. Remember that you may need to change the spelling of the noun; -e changes to -i, for example.
able → ability
responsible → responsibility

Suffix -ist You can form other personal nouns from a noun by adding the suffix -ist. First you need to change the noun, though. For words ending in -cs, take away *cs* and then add -ist. For words ending in -y, take away *y* and then add -ist.
economics → economist
sociology → sociologist

Suffixes -r, -er Add -r or -er to form some personal nouns.
manage → manager
paint → painter
train → trainer

Suffixes -ment, -ion
You can form nouns from verbs in several ways, but note that you may also need to change the base verb before you add the suffix.
entertain → entertainment
inform → information
imagine → imagination

Gerunds Add -ing to form gerunds (the noun form of a verb) but again you may need to change the base verb.
go → going
read → reading
shine → shining
swim → swimming

Multiple-choice cloze (3)

Test it ✔

1 **Match a–k to 1–11.**

a	There was a bank robbery	1	for spinach – it's horrible!	a	...3...
b	James was making a lot	2	as much about it as you do.	b	....
c	Dad's always losing his	3	in the town centre last night.	c	....
d	Pete doesn't dislike you. On	4	each other in total disbelief.	d	....
e	Alison's sad. She misses her	5	his way to the airport.	e	....
f	Laura knows just	6	whenever you like.	f	....
g	Phil said he'd call me on	7	husband a lot.	g	....
h	Please feel free to call me	8	wallet and car keys.	h	....
i	It was interesting that Jo had	9	the contrary, he loves you!	i	....
j	The two girls stared at	10	of noise last night.	j	....
k	I don't like carrots or peas and as	11	such strong opinions on the matter.	k	....

2 **Find and correct the mistakes in the sentences.**

	It's a strange place with as ~~much~~ sheep as there are people.	...many...
a	Paddy told to me a really funny joke.	....
b	I wish you'd stop doing a fuss. It's really not important enough.	....
c	Why won't you say me you love me?	....
d	The house was mugged at approximately 11.30 p.m.	....
e	It can be a spider – it's black, hairy and has eight legs.	....
f	If you're worried about it, we can do a chat.	....
g	It's time we talked to ourselves and sorted the problem out.	....
h	You mustn't be serious! You're joking, aren't you?	....
i	My flat is next the church on West 23rd Street.	....
j	Whoever you look at it, it's still a lot of money to spend.	....
k	Oh, no! My mobile's been robbed!	....
l	And as with the traffic, it's a complete nightmare during rush hour.	....

22

GO to page 48 and check your answers.

Test it again ✔

Read the text below and decide which answer (A, B, C or D) best fits each space.

A LIFE IN THE COUNTRY

One thing I have never understood is the desire to live in the country. People associate life in the city with crime and noise and they (1) .... the impression that life in the country (2) .... be safer and quieter. (3) .... the contrary, country life has (4) .... as many hazards as the big city. I have a friend who lives (5) .... to a farm and he (6) .... that it's noisier living there than it ever was in London. The birds and animals start (7) .... a noise first thing in the morning, quickly followed by the farm machinery. And (8) .... crime, my friend's car has been (9) .... four times in four years. People who think the country is the safest place to be (10) .... be right!

The other myth is that the countryside is a friendly place. (11) .... I spend time in the country, I'm surprised by how busy people are. They never seem to speak to (12) .... for more than a minute or two. On my (13) .... back from work, I often come across three or four neighbours and we (14) .... a long chat. It's that connection with other people that I would (15) .... most if I lived in the country.

1	A show	B have	C make	D take
2	A can't	B has	C must	D mustn't
3	A With	B In	C On	D By
4	A still	B many	C not	D just
5	A by	B between	C next	D beside
6	A wonders	B says	C tells	D asks
7	A doing	B shouting	C giving	D making
8	A as for	B as with	C as of	D as in
9	A mugged	B stolen	C robbed	D burgled
10	A can	B won't	C can't	D will
11	A Whoever	B However	C Whenever	D Whatever
12	A each	B each other	C themselves	D their
13	A way	B route	C street	D direction
14	A make	B have	C do	D talk
15	A avoid	B lose	C forget	D miss

15

🔧 Fix it

Answers to Test it

Check your answers. Wrong answer?
Read the right Fix it note to find out why.

1
a 3	→	B
b 10	→	C
c 8	→	G
d 9	→	E
e 7	→	G
f 2	→	E
g 5	→	C
h 6	→	D
i 11	→	F
j 4	→	D
k 1	→	E

2
• ~~much~~ many	→ E
a ~~told to me~~ told me	→ A
b ~~doing~~ making	→ C
c ~~say me~~ tell me/say	→ A
d ~~mugged~~ burgled	→ B
e ~~can be~~ must be	→ A
f ~~do~~ have	→ C
g ~~ourselves~~ each other	→ D
h ~~mustn't be~~ can't be	→ A
i ~~next~~ next to	→ F
j ~~Whoever~~ However	→ D
k ~~robbed~~ stolen	→ B
l ~~as with~~ as for	→ E

Now go to page 47. Test yourself again.

Answers to Test it again

1 B	9 B
2 C	10 C
3 C	11 C
4 D	12 B
5 C	13 A
6 B	14 B
7 D	15 D
8 A	

🔧 Fix it notes

A Use *must be* and *can't be* to make logical deductions about the present. In reported speech, either use *say + that* or *to + pronoun/name*, or use *tell + pronoun/name*.

B You *steal* things, you *rob* a person or place, and you *burgle* a building. To *mug* is to attack and rob a person in the street.

C Use *make* to talk about things you create, and in a lot of fixed expressions, e.g. *make a noise*. Use *have + object* in certain fixed expressions, e.g. *have an impression, an opinion, a thought, a chat*.

D Use *each other* (not *ourselves* or *themselves*) when people do the same thing. Don't confuse *however, whenever, wherever*, etc. Look at the question word that goes before *-ever*.

E Use *on the contrary* to introduce an opposite opinion or thought. Use *just as much/many* to say that two things are equal. Use *as for* to introduce another subject. *As for* often suggests a dislike of something.

F Use *on the, my, our* etc. *way* to say that something happens during a journey or while moving. *Next to* means 'beside'.

G You *miss* people and things when you no longer have them. If you *miss* something, you regret no longer having it. You *lose* a person or object when you can't find them.

For more information, see the Review page opposite. ▷

i Review

EXAM TIP

- In part 1 of paper 3 only one of the four options, A–D, is correct. Don't mark more than one letter on the answer sheet.
- Don't be influenced by the frequency of As, Bs, etc. in the answers across the task. Base your answer on the meaning and grammar of the sentence.

See page 86 for a description of this part of the Use of English paper.

Must/can't be You use *must be* and *can't be* to make deductions about the present. *You must be tired after your journey. She can't be out. I've just spoken to her.*

Say and *tell* In reported speech, you can use *say* + that or *say to* + pronoun/name. *They said that they enjoyed the film. What did you say to James?*

You use *tell* + pronoun/name. *Tell me when you are ready. Tell Kim your joke.*

⚠ You can't use *tell to* + pronoun/name. *What did she say to you?* NOT ~~*What did she tell to you?*~~

Crime *Steal*, *rob* and *burgle* all mean 'take without permission'. You *steal* things. You *rob* a person or a place. You *burgle* a building. *To mug* is to attack and rob a person in the street. *My mobile was stolen last night. What did you do when you were robbed? Five men robbed the bank. He burgled thirty houses in one year. The woman was mugged and the man took her bag.*

Miss and *lose* You *miss* people and things when you regret no longer having them. *I'll miss you when you're away. I sold my car but I really missed it.*

You *lose* a person or object when you can't find them. *I'm always losing my house keys.*

Make and *have* You use *make* to talk about things you create. You also use *make* in fixed expressions, e.g. *make a noise*. *I've made a cake. Please don't make a mess.*

You use *have* + object in certain fixed expressions, e.g. *have a good time/a meal. Did you have a good time at the party?*

Make a note of common expressions with verbs like *have*, *do*, *make*, etc. and try to learn them as you go along.

Each other and *themselves* You use *each other* when two or more people do the same thing. You use *themselves* (and other reflexive pronouns) when the subject and object of a verb are the same. *The girls smiled at each other. The children hurt themselves.*

However, etc. You add *-ever* to question words like *how, when, where* to mean 'it doesn't matter how/when/where'. Don't confuse these words in the exam. Look at the question word that goes before *-ever* and use the context to help you. *We can meet wherever you like.*

On the contrary You use *on the contrary* to introduce an opposite opinion. *'It was a very good play.' 'On the contrary, the performances were awful.'*

As for You use *as for* to introduce another subject. As for often suggests a dislike of something. *As for the staff, they were very rude.*

Just as much/many You use *just as much/many* to say that two things are the same or equal. *I've got just as many problems as you.*

Prepositions You use *on the, my, our,* etc. *way* to say that something happens during a journey or while moving. *Next to* means 'beside'. Don't forget to include *to*. *I saw an accident on my way home. Come and sit next to me.* NOT ~~*Come and sit next me.*~~

Open cloze (3)

Test it ✔

1 **Circle the correct option.**

Not only (do they sell)/sell they everything you need, it's also good value.
a   I told you! Your glasses are in a/the kitchen.
b   Both my brother and I love listening to/listening RnB and hip hop.
c   We couldn't go swimming because/because of the pollution.
d   Mrs Jones is the woman what/that lives next door to me.
e   The head teacher refuses to put up/put up with bad behaviour.
f   No sooner I had/had I left the room than the baby began to cry.
g   If you hadn't got up so late, we didn't/wouldn't have missed the train.
h   How much/many money do you want?
i   The sky's getting darker and dark/darker.
j   Because/Because of I'm a writer, I spend a lot of time at the computer.

2 **Find and correct ten mistakes in the phone conversation.**

Hello, Jill? It's Jackie here. I'm so glad I've got through to you.
Please listen me. I really need to talk you. Yesterday was one   ......listen to.........
of the silliest days of my life. It just got sillier and sillier as the   ....
day went on. When I hadn't seen my boyfriend, it would have   ....
been OK. I did see him, though. Not only I saw him but I   ....
crashed his lovely new car into a tree! I just reversed it without   ....
look first. Poor Nick really puts up with a lot of nonsense from   ....
me and he's extremely patient. He even says he loves me   ....
because of I'm silly. Isn't that sweet? Anyway, it wasn't just   ....
the car what was a problem that day. Are you still listening, ...
Jill? Much other things went wrong for me. Next, I decided   ....
to go shopping. You know a shop at the end of George Street?   ....
The nice food shop that sells cheese and fresh fruit. Well, ...
I already finished my shopping when I realized that I'd left my   ....
bag and all my money at home. Can you believe it? The shop   ....
assistant and all the customers were laughing me. It was   ....
terrible! Jill? Jill? Are you still there? Jill?   ....

20

GO to page 52 and check your answers.

Test it again ✔

Read the text below and think of the word which best fits each space.
Use only one word in each space.

CAT-ASTROPHE!

I once read an article in which (1) .... author described the terrible things her pets got up to. The poor woman had to put up (2) .... chewed furniture, fur everywhere, and 'accidents' on her carpets. It was her own fault, though. Not only (3) .... she have various furry and feathered friends, she also had a pet alligator (4) .... lived in the bath.

One by one the animals came. At first they were small: a tortoise, a rabbit and a guinea pig. But as time passed, the animals she adopted began to get (5) .... and bigger. First there were cats and dogs, then a goat, an alligator, and finally a llama. The neighbours began to laugh (6) .... Mrs Higgins. Many people disapproved (7) .... her. This was mostly (8) .... they thought her house wasn't suitable for so (9) .... wildlife.

Without (10) .... it, this animal-loving woman (11) .... allowed her house to turn (12) .... a mini zoo. This (13) .... not really have mattered (14) .... she had lived in a large country house, or on a farm, but the fact was that Mrs Higgins and her seventy-three pets (15) .... in a one-bedroom house with a tiny garden in central London.

15

🔧 Fix it

Answers to Test it

Check your answers. Wrong answer?
Read the right Fix it note to find out why.

1
- do they sell → H
- a the → A
- b listening to → F
- c because of → E
- d that → D
- e put up with → C
- f had I → H
- g wouldn't → G
- h much → B
- i darker → E
- j Because → E

2
- ~~listen~~ listen to → F
- a ~~talk~~ talk to → F
- b ~~When~~ If → G
- c ~~I saw~~ did I see → H
- d ~~look~~ looking → F
- e ~~because of~~ because → E
- f ~~what~~ that → D
- g ~~Much~~ Many → B
- h ~~a~~ the → A
- i ~~already~~ had already → G
- j ~~laughing~~ laughing at → F

Now go to page 51. Test yourself again.

Answers to Test it again

1 the
2 with
3 did
4 that/which/who
5 bigger
6 at/about
7 of
8 because
9 much
10 realizing/intending/noticing/
 knowing
11 had
12 into
13 would
14 if
15 lived/were/stayed/remained

🔧 Fix it notes

A Use the definite article *the* when it's obvious which person or thing you're talking about.

B Use *much* and *how much* with uncountable nouns. Use *many* and *how many* with plural nouns.

C Some phrasal verbs have just one preposition or an adverb after them, e.g. *turn into*; others have two, e.g. *put up with*.

D This sentence includes a defining relative clause. Begin these clauses with *who* or *that* for people and *that* or *which* for objects/animals.

E Use *because* before subject + verb. Use *because of* before a noun or pronoun. Use the same comparative adjective twice to say that a situation is changing or developing.

F Use an *-ing* form after a preposition. Some verbs are followed by a preposition, e.g. *laugh at, listen to*.

G Use the past perfect in the *if* clause of third conditional sentences and *would/wouldn't have* in the other clause. Use the past perfect, not the past simple, for a past action which happens before another past action.

H Reverse the position of the subject and auxiliary verb (*be, have, do, can, will*, etc.) after these expressions when they come at the beginning of a sentence: *not only, rarely, no sooner, hardly*. If there's no auxiliary, use a form of *do*.

For more information, see the Review page opposite. ▷

ⓘ Review

EXAM TIP
- In part 2 of paper 3 remember that sometimes more than one answer is possible, but you should write only one word for each gap on the answer sheet.
- Read the whole text through when you have finished to check your answers.

See page 86 for a description of this part of the Use of English paper.

Articles Use the definite article *the* when it's obvious which person or thing you're talking about. The person you're talking to knows what you're referring to.
Nick's in the garden. (the garden of our house)
In the book I'm reading, the writer says that animals can talk. (the writer of the book)

Quantifiers You use *much* and *how much* with uncountable nouns, e.g. *bread, water, news, advice.* You use *many* and *how many* with plural nouns, e.g. *people, books, problems.*
There isn't much bread left.
How many people shall we invite?

Phrasal verbs Some phrasal verbs have just one preposition or an adverb after them, e.g. *turn into*; others have two, e.g. *put up with.* If you're not sure, check in a good dictionary, such as the *Oxford Advanced Learner's Dictionary.*

Relative clauses Begin defining relative clauses with *who* or *that* for people, *that* or *which* for objects, and *where* for a place.
There's the man who stole my bag!
Here's the book that I want you to read.

Because (of) You use *because* before a subject + verb, and *because of* before a noun or pronoun.
I said 'I love you' because I do!
I love him because of his kindness.

Comparatives You use the same comparative adjective twice to say that a situation is changing or developing.
This pile of work is getting bigger and bigger!
The sun became hotter and hotter.

Verb patterns You use an *-ing* form (or a noun) after a preposition, e.g. *in, without, from, under.*
He stopped me from making a fool of myself.

⚠ Some verbs are followed by a preposition that goes before the object of the sentence. If there's no object, you don't use a preposition.
You aren't listening to me! Listen!
NOT *You aren't listening me! Listen to!*
Look at that wonderful rainbow! Just look!

Third conditional You use the past perfect in the *if*-clause of third conditional sentences and *would/wouldn't have* in the other clause.
If I hadn't got up early, I wouldn't have seen the beautiful sunrise.

Past perfect You use the past perfect, not the past simple, for a past action which happens before another past action.
When we arrived at the station, the train had left. (First the train left; then we arrived.)

Inversion You reverse the position of the subject and auxiliary verb (*be, have, do, can, will, must, may*, etc.) after these expressions when they come at the beginning of a sentence: *not only, rarely, no sooner, hardly.* This is formal language and you use it to give emphasis. If there's no auxiliary verb, you use a suitable form of *do.*
Not only was she wearing bright red shoes, she also had a green hat and purple trousers on. (She was wearing bright red shoes, a green hat and purple trousers, and that surprised me.)
Not only did I see my favourite actor, I spoke to him, too! (I saw my favourite actor and I spoke to him.)

Key word transformations (3)

Test it ✔

1 **Circle the correct option.**

I won't go **unless**/except you come with me.
a Jim **managed to/could** read by the time he was four.
b I went to the bank in order to **getting/get** some cash.
c You **used to/would** have long hair, didn't you?
d It's not fair! Mum won't **make/let** me watch TV.
e The burglars **could/managed to** break in even though the door was locked.
f My brother isn't **so/as** clever as I am.
g Is this exercise more difficult **as/than** the last one?
h We went quietly upstairs so that we **didn't/can't** wake anyone up.
i Why do you always **let/make** me do the washing up? I hate it!
j Everything's organized. We **are meeting/will meet** our friends at 7.30.

2 **Choose the correct words and phrases to complete the sentences.**

*going to   if   manage   let   would   couldn't   so that   as
used to   than   in order to*

Ed ...*used to*............ be an accountant. Now he's an actor.
a You're older .... me. (I'm not as old as you.)
b We ran .... we could catch the bus. (We ran because we wanted to catch the bus.)
c Pat .... find his wallet. (Pat wasn't able to find his wallet.)
d He won't invite you .... you don't ask him to. (He won't invite you unless you ask him to.)
e I'm .... see the doctor tomorrow. (I'm seeing the doctor tomorrow.)
f Why won't you .... me speak? (Why won't you allow me to speak?)
g You have to revise .... pass the test. (If you want to pass the test, you have to revise.)
h It wasn't .... difficult as Mike expected. (It was easier than Mike expected.)
i Did you .... to find Joe? (Did you find Joe?)
j We .... often go for walks on the beach. (We often used to go for walks on the beach.)

[ ] 20

GO to page 56 and check your answers.

Test it again ✔

Complete the second sentence so that it has a similar meaning to the first sentence, using the word given. Do not change the word given. You must use between two and five words, including the word given.

1   Shane isn't as tall as Neil.
    than
    Neil .... Shane.

2   Natalie can dance, sing and act.
    able
    Natalie .... dance, sing and act.

3   We're meeting our friends at 9.00.
    going
    We .... our friends at 9.00.

4   I left quietly so that I didn't wake the baby.
    order
    I left quietly .... wake the baby.

5   My mum forced me to tidy my bedroom.
    made
    My mum .... my bedroom.

6   They won't pass the exam if they don't revise.
    unless
    They won't pass the exam ....

7   When I was a kid, I would often spend hours reading.
    used
    When I was a kid, I often .... hours reading.

8   It took a long time but we succeeded in fixing the car.
    managed
    It took a long time but we .... the car.

9   The librarian allowed me to borrow three books.
    let
    The librarian .... three books.

10 The book was better than the film.
    as
    The film .... the book.

20

⚒ Fix it

Answers to Test it

Check your answers. Wrong answer?
Read the right Fix it note to find out why.

1
- unless → E
- **a** could → B
- **b** get → D
- **c** used to → F
- **d** let → G
- **e** managed to → B
- **f** as → A
- **g** than → A
- **h** didn't → D
- **i** make → G
- **j** are meeting → C

2
- used to → F
- **a** than → A
- **b** so that → D
- **c** couldn't → B
- **d** if → E
- **e** going to → C
- **f** let → G
- **g** in order to → D
- **h** as → A
- **i** manage → B
- **j** would → F

◀ Now go to page 55. Test yourself again.

Answers to Test it again

(2 marks for each correct sentence)
1 's/is taller than
2 's/is able to
3 're/are going to meet
4 in order not to
5 made me tidy
6 unless they revise
7 used to spend
8 managed to fix
9 let me borrow
10 wasn't/was not as good as

⚒ Fix it notes

A Use *than* after a comparative adjective. Use (*not*) *as* + adjective + *as to* to say that two things are the same as each other or different from each other.

B Use *can, could, be* + *able to* and *manage to* to talk about ability. Use *managed to* or *was/were able to* + base verb to talk about ability on a particular occasion in the past.

C Use *going to* to talk about general plans you've made for the future. Also use the present continuous to talk about fixed plans and arrangements you've made, especially when you mention a time or place.

D Use *in order to* + base form. The negative is *in order not to* + base form. Use *so* (*that*) + modal verb. In the negative, use a form of the verb *do* or a modal verb, e.g. ... *so* (*that*) *I didn't/wouldn't* ... .

E *Unless* means the same as *if not* or *except if*.

F Use *used to* + base form to talk about things that happened in the past but don't happen now. Use *would* + base form for past repeated actions or habits. Don't use *would* with state verbs. Use the past simple or *used to* instead.

G Use *make* + noun or pronoun + base form when someone forces someone else to do something. Use *let* + noun or pronoun + base form when someone allows someone else to do something.

For more information, see the Review page opposite. ▷

ℹ️ Review

EXAM TIP

- In part 3 of paper 3 don't change the meaning of the first sentence by leaving out important words in the second sentence.
- Don't change the key word in any way.
- Make sure you use between two and five words (including the key word) to complete the sentence. Contractions, e.g. *I'm*, count as two words.

See page 86 for a description of this part of the Use of English paper.

Comparatives You use *than* (not *that*) after a comparative adjective. You use (*not*) *as* + adjective + *as* to say that two things are the same as each other or different from each other.
Your car's a lot faster than mine.
My car's not as fast as yours.

Ability You use *can, could, be able to* and *manage to* to talk about ability. Usually you use *can* to talk about general ability. You use *managed to* or *was/were able to* + base verb to talk about ability on a particular occasion in the past. You often use *managed to* when a situation was particularly difficult.
Can you understand these instructions?
Were you able to speak French when you were a child?
We were lost and it was dark but we managed to find our way home.

Future plans and intentions You use *going to* to talk about general plans that you have already made for the future. You can also use the present continuous to talk about fixed plans and arrangements you have made for the future, especially when you mention a time or place.
I'm going to ask for a pay rise.
I'm seeing the doctor at 9.15 tomorrow.

⚠️ When the verb *go* follows *going to*, you often leave it out.
I'm going to go to the supermarket later.
→ *I'm going to the supermarket later.*

In order (not) to You can use *in order to* + base form of the verb to say why someone does something. You use *in order not to* as the negative form.
He took a taxi in order to save time.
Take regular exercise in order not to put on weight.

So (that) You usually use *so* or *so that* with a modal verb such as *can, will*, etc. to say why someone does something. In the negative, you use a form of the verb *do* or a modal verb.
I shouted so (that) they could hear me.
NOT ~~I shouted so that they heard me.~~
Wear a jacket so (that) you don't get cold.
NOT ~~Wear a jacket so that not get cold.~~

Unless You can use *unless* with the same meaning as 'if not' or 'except if'.
We'll be late unless we hurry. = *If we don't hurry, we'll be late.*

Used to and *would* You use *used to* + base form to talk about things that happened in the past but don't happen now. You use *would* + base form for past repeated actions or habits.
I used to be a teacher, but now I work in marketing.
As a child, I would play on the beach for hours.

Don't use *would* with state verbs (*love, know, have*, etc.), use the past simple or *used to* instead.
I used to have long hair but I don't now.
NOT ~~I would have long hair.~~

Make and *let* You use *make* + noun/pronoun + base form when someone forces someone else to do something. You use *let* + noun/pronoun + base form when someone allows someone else to do something.
Don't make the dog do tricks. He doesn't like it.
Why won't you let me stay up late?

Test it ✔

① **Find and correct six mistakes. Cross out the extra words.**

It's a film about the fight between good and ~~the~~ evil.

a   I told to him my name.
b   You're such a good friend.
c   The most important thing to me is an honesty.
d   If we'll have time, we'll meet Jo for a drink.
e   How did you cut yourself?
f   Give me a ring before you will go tomorrow.
g   Why didn't you answer my question?
h   Did you let your brother borrow your car?
i   Were you at the home yesterday evening?
j   I heard a worrying news about the company.

② **True or false?**

	TRUE	FALSE
A The bed cost £300 and the sofa cost £200. **B** I always fall asleep when I read in the bed. Neither of these sentences is possible.	☐	☑
a **A** I've given to him the money. **B** We've lent the car to him. Both of these sentences are possible.	☐	☐
b **A** What did Kathy ask to you? **B** My neighbour asked me what time it was. Only one of these sentences is possible.	☐	☐
c **A** Call me when you will get home this evening. **B** Have fun when you go to Paris next month. Only one of these sentences is possible.	☐	☐
d **A** I gave up of smoking last year. **B** I'm working. I can't put up with this noise! Neither of these sentences is possible.	☐	☐
e **A** Who's the most oldest member of your family? **B** That was the best meal I've ever eaten. Only one of these sentences is possible.	☐	☐

15

GO to page 60 and check your answers.

Test it again ✔

Read the text below and look carefully at each line. Some of the lines are correct, and some have a word which should not be there. If a line is correct, put a tick (✓) next to it. If a line has a word that should not be there, cross it out.

A THANK YOU LETTER

1   Thank you for your birthday card. It was very kind of you to
2   send to me a present. I had a fantastic time on my birthday.
3   We went to one of the nicest restaurants in town. I tried
4   oysters for the first time, but I don't think I would have of them
5   again. Mum and Dad had invited all the family to dinner
6   so that made ten of us altogether. The waiter said we were the most
7   noisiest group they have ever had! Can I ask for you a favour?
8   When shall you next see your brother, please ask him for the names
9   of some good hotels in New York. I need an information on places to
10 stay in Manhattan and he used to live there, didn't he? Tell him
11 not to worry about location – the most important thing to me is the
12 friendliness. Before I will go on holiday, I'll give you a ring.
13 When will you be at the home? Perhaps we can meet up
14 of and go to the cinema, or we could have a meal if you like.
15 Please say hello to all your family from me. Speak to you soon.

15

🔧 Fix it

Answers to Test it

Check your answers. Wrong answer?
Read the right Fix it note to find out why.

1
- and ~~the~~ evil → C
- a told ~~to~~ him → B
- b correct
- c is ~~an~~ honesty → C
- d we'~~ll~~ have → E
- e correct
- f you ~~will~~ go → E
- g correct
- h correct
- i at ~~the~~ home → D
- j heard ~~a~~ worrying → C

2
- • False → D
- a False → A
- b True → B
- c True → E
- d False → F
- e True → G

> Now go to page 59. Test yourself again.

Answers to Test it again

- 1 ✔
- 2 ~~to~~
- 3 ✔
- 4 ~~of~~
- 5 ✔
- 6 ~~most~~
- 7 ~~for~~
- 8 ~~shall~~
- 9 ~~an~~
- 10 ✔
- 11 is ~~the~~
- 12 ~~will~~
- 13 ~~the~~
- 14 ~~of~~
- 15 ✔

🔧 Fix it notes

A Usually put the indirect object before (not after) the direct object. Don't use *to* + indirect object + direct object.

B Don't use *to* after the verbs *ask* and *tell*. Always put an object pronoun or someone's name.

C Don't use *a, an, the* with abstract nouns, e.g. *honesty, love.* Don't use *a* or *an* with uncountable nouns, e.g. *news, information.*

D Don't use an article with some common expressions, e.g. *at school, at home, at work, in hospital, in bed.*

E Don't use *will/won't* in the *if*-clause in first conditional sentences. Use the present tense. Use the present simple after *when* and *before* to talk about the future.

F Some phrasal verbs have just one preposition or an adverb after them, e.g. *give up*; others have two, e.g. *put up with.*

G Don't use *most* with the superlative form of one-syllable adjectives.

> For more information, see the Review page opposite.

ⓘ Review

Direct and indirect objects When the verb in a sentence has two objects, you usually put the indirect object before (not after) the direct object. An indirect object is often a person, and a direct object is often a thing.
Sam gave the kids a new toy.
In this sentence 'a new toy' is the direct object; 'the kids' is the indirect object.
You can also put the indirect object before the direct object but you usually need to add *to* or *for*.
I've given the money to John.
We bought some flowers for Mum.
In these sentences, 'the money' and 'some flowers' are the indirect objects; 'John' and 'Mum' are the direct objects.

⚠ Don't use *to* + indirect object + direct object.
I've given John the money.
NOT ~~I've given to John the money.~~

Ask and tell You don't use *to* + person after the verbs *ask* and *tell*. You most often put an object pronoun (*me, him, us*, etc.) or someone's name after *ask*. You always put a person's name or object pronoun after the verb *tell*.
Eileen asked me what I thought.
NOT ~~Eileen asked to me ...~~
Tell Paul to come and see us.

First conditional You use the present tense (not *will/won't*) in the *if*-clause in first conditional sentences.
If it's sunny, we'll play tennis.
NOT ~~If it will be sunny, we'll play tennis.~~

Present simple You use the present simple after *when* and *before* to talk about the future.
Please call me when you get home.
NOT ~~Please call me when you will get home.~~

Phrasal verbs Some phrasal verbs have just one preposition or an adverb after them, e.g. *give up*; others have two, e.g. *put up with*. If you're not sure, check in a good dictionary, such as the *Oxford Advanced Learner's Dictionary*.

Articles Abstract nouns are things you can't see or touch, like *love, honesty, peace*, etc. When you're talking about these things in general, don't use *a, an* or *the*. Also don't use *a, an* or *the* with these common expressions: *at school, at home, at work, in hospital, in bed.*
All you need is love. NOT ~~All you need is the love.~~
Joe's at school and Bob's at home.

You don't use *a* or *an* with uncountable nouns, e.g. *news, information, advice, money.*
We need information about flights to Bangkok. NOT ~~an information~~

Superlatives You form the superlative of one-syllable adjectives with *-est* (not *most*).
Granny was the oldest person at the wedding.
Which is the coldest month?

Test it ✔

❶ Circle the correct option, A or B.

They say that a .... glass of red wine is good for you.
A dayly   **Ⓑ** daily

a What's your most vivid .... memory?
A childish   **B** childhood

b I'd like to .... the colour of my hair.
A lighter   **B** lighten

c My family is of great .... to me.
A importance   **B** important

d .... of an animal is big responsibility.
A Ownership   **B** Ownerness

e The .... version of the poem was quite good.
A translator   **B** translated

f Exposure to the hot sun can be very ....
A harmful   **B** harmless

❷ Complete the sentences. Use the correct form of the words in brackets.

I've never seen such ...*brilliance*............... (brilliant) on a football pitch!

a The meeting was really .... (produce) – we didn't achieve anything.

b Do you think our team will win the .... (champion)?

c It's important to wear .... (protect) clothing when dealing with chemicals.

d Please send us the .... (revise) plans for the new school building.

e The curtains are a bit short. Can you .... (long) them?

f I don't see the .... (relevant) of what you are saying.

g I thought that the singers in the show were really .... (impress) – their voices were awful.

h We have a .... (week) progress meeting.

i My sister is finding .... (mother) difficult – she isn't enjoying being a parent.

j My friend is a .... (success) painter – he sells a lot of his work in galleries around the country.

16

GO to page 64 and check your answers.

Test it again ✔

Read the text below. Use the word given in capitals at the end of each line to form a word that fits in the space in the same line.

A FRIEND FOR LIFE

It's surprising how (1) …. changes. When people are young, they **FRIEND**
have a large number of friends with whom they are in (2) …. contact. **DAY**
As teenagers, they often become more (3) …. and their circle of **SELECT**
friends is normally smaller. However, the (4) …. of friends and **IMPORTANT**
(5) …. grows. Teenagers often prefer to confide in a best friend, while **RELATION**
being completely (6) …. with all adults. Later, people develop different **COMMUNICATE**
'levels' of friends. Their circle of friends starts to (7) …. and they have **BROAD**
different groups to relate to – those who live in their (8) …. , colleagues, **NEIGHBOUR**
people they just say 'hi' to, along with family and (9) …. close friends. **ESTABLISH**
Retirement is ideally a (10) …. time, with friends often being reunited **JOY**
across the years. At any stage in life, friends help and support us,
and often know us best.

1 FRIEND	……………………………	**6** COMMUNICATE	……………………………
2 DAY	……………………………	**7** BROAD	……………………………
3 SELECT	……………………………	**8** NEIGHBOUR	……………………………
4 IMPORTANT	……………………………	**9** ESTABLISH	……………………………
5 RELATION	……………………………	**10** JOY	……………………………

☐ 10

🔧 Fix it

Answers to Test it

Check your answers. Wrong answer?
Read the right Fix it note to find out why.

1
- • B → B
- a B → A
- b B → E
- c A → D
- d A → A
- e B → F
- f A → G

2
- • brilliance → D
- a unproductive → C
- b championship → A
- c protective → C
- d revised → F
- e lengthen → E
- f relevance → D
- g unimpressive → C
- h weekly → B
- i motherhood → A
- j successful → G

Now go to page 63. Test yourself again.

Answers to Test it again

1 friendship
2 daily
3 selective
4 importance
5 relationships
6 uncommunicative
7 broaden
8 neighbourhood
9 established
10 joyful

🔧 Fix it notes

A To make an abstract noun from some other nouns, add *-ship* or *-hood*, e.g. *relation* → *relationship*, *neighbour* → *neighbourhood*.

B To make an adjective from a noun that is a period of time, add *-ly*, e.g. *week* → *weekly*. Remember that you may have to make a spelling change, e.g. *day* → *daily*.

C To make an adjective from some verbs, add *-ive*, e.g. *select* → *selective*. To make the opposite of some adjectives, add *un-*, e.g. *communicative* → *uncommunicative*.

D To make a noun from some adjectives, use *-ance*, e.g. *important* → *importance*.

E To make a verb from some adjectives, add *-en*, e.g. *broad* → *broaden*. You may need to make a spelling change, e.g. *long* → *lengthen*.

F Past participles can be used as adjectives, often with a passive sense. To make a past participle from a regular verb, add *-d* or *-ed*, e.g. *prepare* → *prepared*, *establish* → *established*.

G To make a positive adjective from some nouns, add *-ful*, e.g. *joy* → *joyful*.

For more information, see the Review page opposite.

ℹ Review

Abstract nouns You can make an abstract noun from some other nouns, by adding *-ship* or *-hood*, e.g. *relation* ➜ *relationship*; *neighbour* ➜ *neighbourhood*. Some common nouns with these suffixes include: *censorship, citizenship, friendship, membership, partnership, ownership, scholarship; childhood, mother/fatherhood.*

Adjectives from nouns You can make an adjective from a noun that is a period of time, by adding *-ly*, e.g. *week* ➜ *weekly* (every week), *year* ➜ *yearly* (every year). Remember that you may have to make a spelling change, e.g. *day* ➜ *daily*.

You can make a positive adjective from some nouns by adding the suffix *-ful*, e.g. *joy* ➜ *joyful, hope* ➜ *hopeful*. Again, you may need to make some spelling changes, e.g. *beauty* ➜ *beautiful*.

Opposite adjectives You can make the opposite of many adjectives, add the prefix *un-*, e.g. *communicative* ➜ *uncommunicative, grateful* ➜ *ungrateful, happy* ➜ *unhappy*.

Nouns from adjectives You can make a noun from some adjectives by using the suffix *-ance*, e.g. *important* ➜ *importance, relevant* ➜ *relevance, significant* ➜ *significance*. Remember that you may need to change the spelling and/or drop some letters before adding the suffix.

Adjectives from verbs You can make an adjective from some verbs by adding *-ive*, e.g. *select* ➜ *selective, create* ➜ *creative, invent* ➜ *inventive*.

Verbs from adjectives You can make a verb from some adjectives by adding *-en*, e.g. *broad* ➜ *broaden*. Be careful because you need to make changes in some words, e.g. *long* ➜ *lengthen*.

Past participles as adjectives You can use some past participles as adjectives, often with a passive meaning. To make a past participle from a regular verb, you add *-d* or *-ed*, e.g. *prepare* ➜ *prepared, establish* ➜ *established*.
This is a translated version of Loepardi's poems.
Joe is an established member of the group.

Multiple-choice cloze (4)

Test it ✔

1 Choose the correct words to complete the sentences. There are five words you don't need.

anything   made   in   going   nothing   achieve   to   win did   memoirs   of   memories   beat   something   lots several   ~~gain~~   go   succeed   few   none

Lots of people ......*gain*............ weight as they get older.

a   There are a .... good films out at the moment.

b   Get up! There's .... wrong with you so stop being lazy.

c   Nick .... his best in the exam but he only just passed.

d   Most .... my friends think I'm slightly crazy.

e   One day, I'll get a piece of paper and start writing my ....

f   You'll .... the match! Just go for it!

g   Dan wants to .... skiing next year.

h   The producer went to Boston last week and .... some great business contacts.

i   We both have such good .... of that week in Milan.

j   .... is making a weird noise outside.

k   We're all looking forward .... meeting you next week.

l   You need to work hard to .... your ambitions.

m   .... of my friends likes films as much as I do.

n   .... protestors were arrested during the demonstration.

o   Cathy doesn't believe .... ghosts, witches or fairies.

2 Look at the words in bold and correct the mistakes.

Dietrich's very shy. He doesn't **have** friends very easily.   *make*

a   **Enjoy** a good time at the party!   ....

b   Sheila **did** a lot of mistakes at first but she's good at her job now.   ....

c   I didn't do **nothing** wrong!   ....

d   John has **won** a lot of confidence since he got his new job.   ....

e   We bought some great **memories** when we were in Mexico City.   ....

f   Have you **made** the washing up yet?   ....

g   Steve's always off somewhere. He goes **to hike** every summer.   ....

h   **Most the people** who know Janet like her very much.   ....

i   If you have a **temporary** job, you only work part of the day or week. ....

j   Paul has an MBA so his **skills** for the job are excellent.   ....

25

GO to page 68 and check your answers.

Test it again ✔

Read the text below and decide which answer (A, B, C or D) best fits each space.

THE VALUE OF A GAP YEAR

I'm in my final term at school and I'll be going to university after the summer.
(1) .... my friends have decided to take a gap year, so they won't start their
(2) .... for twelve months. They are convinced that they will (3) .... useful
experience before becoming a student. I'm not so sure.

My sister went (4) .... for six months two years ago. She backpacked around
Australia and travelled home via Asia. She (5) .... a good time, but she
didn't really learn (6) .... Quite the opposite – she thought it was a holiday
and she (7) .... out of the habit of doing routine things. She got up late
every morning, lay on the beach all day, and went (8) .... every night.
She didn't do any part-time (9) .... and so she didn't learn any new
(10) .... She wanted to help people so she was going to do some (11) ....
work but she didn't (12) .... contact with any charities while she was away.
The trip also cost her a fortune – she doesn't (13) .... in travelling light, so
she bought (14) .... everywhere that she stopped.

I hope my schoolmates enjoy their trips, but I'm looking (15) .... to starting
university – the sooner you start, the sooner you finish.

1	**A** Most of	**B** A few	**C** Several	**D** None of
2	**A** employment	**B** study	**C** course	**D** career
3	**A** achieve	**B** win	**C** take	**D** gain
4	**A** traveller	**B** travels	**C** travelling	**D** travel
5	**A** got	**B** had	**C** experienced	**D** enjoyed
6	**A** something	**B** nothing	**C** anyone	**D** anything
7	**A** got	**B** came	**C** was	**D** became
8	**A** danced	**B** to dance	**C** dance	**D** dancing
9	**A** employer	**B** work	**C** employee	**D** job
10	**A** qualifications	**B** training	**C** skills	**D** qualities
11	**A** voluntary	**B** part-time	**C** well-paid	**D** temporary
12	**A** give	**B** make	**C** do	**D** give
13	**A** approve	**B** like	**C** enjoy	**D** believe
14	**A** memoirs	**B** souvenirs	**C** memories	**D** remembrances
15	**A** forward	**B** back	**C** for	**D** up

15

🔧 Fix it

Answers to Test it

Check your answers. Wrong answer? Read the right Fix it note to find out why.

1
•	gain	→	E
a	few	→	A
b	nothing	→	A
c	did	→	C
d	of	→	A
e	memoirs	→	F
f	win	→	E
g	go	→	D
h	made	→	C
i	memories	→	F
j	Something	→	A
k	to	→	B
l	achieve	→	E
m	None	→	A
n	Several	→	A
o	in	→	B

2
•	make	→	C
a	Have	→	D
b	made	→	C
c	anything	→	A
d	gained	→	E
e	souvenirs	→	F
f	done	→	C
g	hiking	→	D
h	Most of the people	→	A
i	part-time	→	F
j	qualifications	→	F

Now go to page 67. Test yourself again.

Answers to Test it again

1	A	9	B
2	C	10	C
3	D	11	A
4	C	12	B
5	B	13	D
6	D	14	B
7	A	15	A
8	D		

🔧 Fix it notes

A Use *most of, none of, a few of, several of* before words like *the, his, that,* etc. Use *several* and *a few* with plural nouns. Use *something* and *nothing* in positive sentences. Use *anything* in questions and negative sentences.

B Form phrasal verbs with one or more short words after the verb. Some verbs are often followed by a preposition.

C Use the verb *do* in some fixed expressions; for things that are connected with work; and before words like *some, any,* etc. followed by *-ing* forms. Use *make* to talk about things you create, and in some fixed expressions, e.g. *make friends*.

D Use *have* + object in certain fixed expressions, e.g. *have a good time*. Often use an *-ing* form after the verb *go*, e.g. *go travelling*.

E Many verbs go with certain words, e.g. *win a game/prize/battle; gain weight/an advantage/confidence*.

F A *memory* is something you remember, a *memoir* is a written account of a memory, a *souvenir* is an object you buy to remind you of a place. A *temporary job* is one you do for a short or fixed time; a *part-time job* is for part of each week. A *voluntary job* is one you don't get paid for. A *course* is a period of study or training. *Qualifications* are a written record of training. *Skills* are things that you can do.

> For more information, see the Review page opposite. ▷

ℹ️ Review

- In part 1 of paper 3 check the whole text when you have finished to make sure you have chosen the correct answers.
- To prepare for this part of the test, it's useful to make a note of vocabulary in context so that you can see how it is used.

See page 86 for a description of this part of the Use of English paper.

Quantifiers You use *most of, none of, a few of, several of* before words like *the, his, that,* etc.
Most of my friends are taking a gap year.

You use *several* and *a few* with plural nouns.
He's had several jobs this year.
A few students failed their final exams.

Something, nothing, etc. You use *something* and *nothing* in positive sentences. You use *anything* in questions and negative sentences.
I'd like to ask you something.
There was nothing I could do.
We couldn't remember anything about it.

Phrasal verbs You form phrasal verbs with one or more short words after the verb. These words change the basic meaning of the verb and you need to learn these new meanings.
You can't look up any words in the exam.
Are you looking forward to your holiday?

Verb + preposition Remember that some verbs are often followed by a preposition.

⚠️ Use *on* (not *of*) after *depend*.
My choice of university depends on the grades I get.

Do and make You use the verb *do* in some fixed expressions and for things that are connected with work.
Have you done the shopping yet?
What job do you do?

You also use *do* before words like *some, any,* etc. followed by *-ing* forms.
We need to do some revising.

You use *make* to talk about things you create, and in a lot of fixed expressions.
We need to make a plan for the project.
Have you made much progress?

Have and go You use *have* + object in certain fixed expressions, e.g. *have lots of fun/a safe trip.* You often use *-ing* form after the verb *go*, e.g. *go travelling.*
Did you have fun at the party?
How often do you go skiing?

Verb + noun Many verbs go with certain words, e.g. *achieve a goal/aim/ambition; win a game/prize/battle; gain weight/an advantage/confidence.* It's a good idea to make a note of these collocations and to revise them regularly.

Remembering things A *memory* is something you remember; a *memoir* is a written account of a memory; a *souvenir* is an object you buy (usually on holiday) to remind you of a place.
I have happy memories of my childhood.
The former prime minister is writing his memoirs.
Let's buy some pottery as a souvenir.

Jobs and training A *temporary job* is one you do for a short or fixed time; a *part-time job* is for part of each week. A *voluntary job* is one you don't get paid for.
I've got a temporary job for six months.

A *course* is a period of study or training. *Qualifications* are a written record of training. *Skills* are things that you can do.
I'm doing a course to improve my computer skills.
I think Emma has the right qualifications for the job.

Open cloze (4)

Test it ✔

1 Solve the clues to complete the crossword.

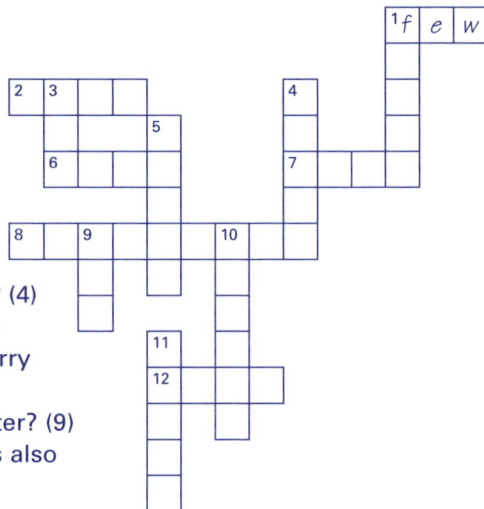

Across

1 Most of us agreed with the manager, but a ..... disagreed. (3)

2 ..... I really need is a long sleep. (4)

6 What ..... you doing a minute ago? (4)

7 They were ..... to getting up early so the five o'clock start didn't worry them. (4)

8 Has your dad ever ..... by helicopter? (9)

12 The house is not ..... small but it's also cold and damp. (4)

Down

1 Wild seals can be ..... on the coast of California. (5)

3 I hadn't realized ..... difficult it was to learn a second language until I tried. (3)

4 We ..... see a large cloud of smoke coming from the building. (5)

5 Are you sure you've ..... been to Vienna? (5)

9 I met the man of my dreams only eleven months ..... . (3)

10 I've only a ..... time before I have to catch my train. (6)

11 I was ..... to email you but I forgot. (5)

2 Find and correct the mistakes in the sentences.

I've been to Bolivia six years ago. ......*went*...........

a Haven't you never tasted chocolate? ....

b No one could predicted that I'd break my leg on holiday. ....

c There's a few money left in that box over there. ....

d That Martha wants most of all is a dog. ....

e We were all surprised by how much pretty she looked. ....

f Philip said he is going to call but he didn't. ....

g That's the girl what loves you most. ....

h The boys were wet because they been swimming. ....

i Your homework must found! ....

j I'm not used to living in such a hot climate but I soon started to enjoy it. ....

22

GO to page 72 and check your answers.

Test it again ✔

**Read the text below and think of the word which best fits each space.
Use only one word in each space.**

A BEAUTIFUL PLACE

One of the most beautiful places I have (1) .... been to is
Andalusia, in the south of Spain. It was a few years (2) ....
when I was visiting a friend (3) .... lived in the area. I had
(4) .... living in the north of Spain for a (5) ....
years but I hadn't yet visited the south of the country. Nothing could
(6) .... prepared me for the differences I (7) ....
going to experience.

The first thing I noticed was the accent of the local people – it was so different
from what I (8) .... used to. (9) .... also hit me
was the change of scenery. Where I lived was beautiful, but I couldn't
(10) .... my eyes when I saw the mountains and coastline of the
region. The third thing that struck me was (11) .... friendly the
people were.

During my stay we went on a trip to the city of Granada. This is
(12) .... a wonderful Moorish palace called the Alhambra can
(13) .... found. It is situated on a hill and consists of three
groups of buildings: the Royal Palace, the palace gardens and the Alcazaba or
fortress. The Alhambra is not only very beautiful, but (14) ....
wonderfully peaceful. I have (15) .... forgotten my time there.

15

⚙ Fix it

Answers to Test it

Check your answers. Wrong answer?
Read the right Fix it note to find out why.

① Across

1 few	→	F
2 What	→	E
6 were	→	A
7 used	→	C
8 travelled	→	A
12 only	→	F

Down

1 found	→	B
3 how	→	F
4 could	→	D
5 never	→	A
9 ago	→	A
10 little	→	F
11 going	→	C

②

• ~~'ve been to~~ went	→	A
a ~~never tasted~~ ever tasted	→	A
b ~~could predicted~~		
could have predicted	→	D
c ~~a few~~ a little/some	→	F
d ~~That~~ What	→	E
e ~~how much~~ how pretty	→	F
f ~~is going to~~ was going to	→	C
g ~~what~~ who/that	→	E
h ~~they been~~ they had been	→	B
i ~~must~~ must be	→	B
j ~~I'm not used to~~		
I wasn't used to	→	C

◀ Now go to page 71. Test yourself again.

◀ Now go to page 71. Test yourself again.

Answers to Test it again

1 ever	9	What
2 ago	10	believe
3 who/that	11	how
4 been	12	where
5 few	13	be
6 have	14	also
7 was	15	never
8 was		

⚙ Fix it notes

A Use the adverbs *ever* and *never* with the present perfect. *Ever* means at any time in your life, *never* means not at any time in your life. Use *ago* with the past simple or continuous, not with the present perfect.

B Form the past perfect continuous with *had been* + *-ing*. Form modals in the present simple passive with *can, must, may,* etc. + *be* + past participle.

C Use *was/were going to* + infinitive to say that something was planned for the future at a time in the past, but that the plan changed. Use *was/were used to* to talk about things that were familiar to you in the past.

D Use *could have* + past participle to say that something was possible but it didn't happen. Use *could/couldn't* + verbs connected with senses and thinking to describe ability on an occasion in the past.

E Use *what* as a relative pronoun when you mean 'the thing or things which …'. Use the relative pronouns *who, that, where* etc. to start relative clauses. Relative pronouns refer to the noun earlier in the sentence.

F Use *a few* with plural nouns, and *a little* with singular (usually uncountable) nouns. Use *how* (not *how much*) before adjectives and adverbs. *Not only… but also…* is a fixed phrase which goes immediately before the words or phrases it's modifying.

For more information, see the Review page opposite. ▷

ℹ️ Review

- To prepare for part 2 of paper 3, make your own tests by taking out grammatical words from a text, e.g. prepositions, articles, pronouns. Exchange tests with another student and check your answers against the original.

See page 86 for a description of this part of the Use of English paper.

Present perfect and past simple You use the adverbs *ever* and *never* with the present perfect, often when talking about experiences. *Ever* means 'at any time in your life', *never* means 'not at any time in your life.' Use an affirmative verb with *never*. *I've never seen a ghost.* NOT ~~I haven't never seen a ghost.~~

You use *ago* with the past simple or continuous, not with the present perfect. *Ago* goes after the time reference. *I started my course three months ago. What were you doing a few hours ago?*

Past perfect continuous You form the past perfect continuous with *had been* + -*ing*. There are sometimes spelling changes when you add -*ing* to the verb. *We'd been driving for hours when the car broke down.*

Passive modals You form modals in the present simple passive with *can, must, may*, etc. + *be* + past participle. *Visitors must be signed in at reception.*

Was/were going to You use *was/were going to* + infinitive to say that something was planned for the future at a time in the past, but that the plan changed. *We were going to buy tickets for the concert but they had sold out.*

was/were used to You use *was/were used to* + -*ing* to mean 'was/were accustomed to' and to talk about things that were familiar to you in the past. *As a dancer, I was used to training hard.*

⚠️ Don't confuse *was/were used to* + -*ing* with *used to*. *We were used to living in the country.* (We were accustomed to it.) *We used to live in the country.* (We lived in the country but we don't now.)

Could have You use *could have* + past participle to say that something was possible but it didn't happen. *It was good that we had the map. We could have got lost without it.*

Could/couldn't You use *could/couldn't* + verbs connected with senses (*see, hear, smell, taste, feel*) and thinking (*remember, understand*) to describe ability on an occasion in the past. *We could hear a strange noise. I saw my old teacher but I couldn't remember his name.*

Relative pronouns You use *what* as a relative pronoun when you mean 'the thing or things which …'. *What I need is a long holiday.*

You use the relative pronouns *who, that, where*, etc. to start relative clauses. They refer to the noun earlier in the sentence. *I'm the man who called earlier.* (*who* = the man) *This is the car that I'm going to buy.* (*that* = the car) *Paris is the city where I met my boyfriend.* (*where* = the city)

Quantifiers You use *a few* with plural nouns, and *a little* with singular (usually uncountable) nouns. *I've got a few letters to write. We've got a little time before the film.*

You use *how* (not *how much*) before adjectives and adverbs. *I couldn't believe how cold it was.* NOT ~~… how much cold it was.~~

Not only … but also … This is a fixed phrase which is used to give emphasis. It goes immediately before the words or phrases it's modifying. *She's not only a singer but also an actress.*

Key word transformations (4)

Test it ✔

① **Which sentence, A or B, means the same as the first sentence?**

I wish I could afford a house. ...A....
  A If only I could afford a house.
  B I used to be able to afford a house.

a I'd rather you didn't say things like that. ....
  A I'd prefer you not to say things like that.
  B I prefer you don't say things like that.

b We can afford to go on holiday. ....
  A We've got too much money to go on holiday.
  B We've got enough money to go on holiday.

c Sue would have caught the train if she hadn't overslept. ....
  A Sue caught the train because she overslept.
  B Sue didn't wake up in time, so she missed the train.

d Someone's bought the house I wanted to buy. ....
  A The house I wanted to buy has been sold.
  B The house I wanted to buy is for sale.

e 'Do you want some more pasta?', asked Michelle. ....
  A Michelle asked did I want some more pasta.
  B Michelle asked if I wanted some more pasta.

② **Correct the second sentence in each pair. Keep the same meaning.**

If only he'd leave. I wish ~~he'll~~ leave. _he'd_ ....

a My car was sold to Tony. Tony was bought my car. ....
b 'What's the time?', he asked. He asked me what was the time. ....
c I wish I hadn't said that. If only I didn't say that. ....
d Patrick would prefer to come for lunch. Patrick rather comes
for lunch. ....
e You're driving too fast. You aren't driving enough slowly. ....
f I'm happy to advise you. I don't mind to advise you. ....
g It isn't necessary for me to go to school. I mustn't go to school. ....
h I don't read enough. I read little too. ....
i 'When will you finish?' He asked when would I finish. ....
j 'If you'd worked harder, you'd have passed the exam.'
'You wouldn't have failed the exam if you aren't so lazy.' ....

15

GO to page 76 and check your answers.

Test it again ✔

Complete the second sentence so that it has a similar meaning to the first sentence, using the word given. Do not change the word given. You must use between two and five words, including the word given.

1   Would you prefer to watch a film or listen to music?
rather
Would .... a film or listen to music?

2   I wouldn't have gone out if I'd known you were coming.
stayed
I .... at home if I'd known you were coming.

3   There really isn't enough milk to make a sauce.
too
There's .... milk to make a sauce.

4   The police arrested Mr Briggs after a short car chase.
was
Mr Briggs .... after a short car chase.

5   'What do you think of the new sports centre?' he asked.
asked
He .... of the new sports centre.

6   The kids can stay at home today as the holiday has started.
have
The kids .... to school today.

7   If only I hadn't fallen in love with you!
wish
I .... in love with you!

8   I'd really like my boss to promote me next year.
would
I .... me next year.

9   I'm happy to teach you how to use the software.
mind
I .... you how to use the software.

10 Would you like to go for a drink tonight?
like
He asked .... to go for a drink that night.

20

🔧 Fix it

Answers to Test it

Check your answers. Wrong answer?
Read the right Fix it note to find out why.

1 • A → A
a A → A
b B → C
c B → B
d A → D
e B → E

2 • he'll he'd → A
a was bought
   bought/was sold → D
b what was the time
   what the time was → E
c didn't say hadn't said → A
d rather comes
   would rather come → A
e enough slowly
   slowly enough → C
f to advise advising → F
g mustn't go
   don't have to go → F
h little too
   too little → C
i would I I would → E
j were had been → B

Now go to page 75. Test yourself again.

Answers to Test it again

(2 marks for each correct sentence)
1 you rather watch
2 'd/would have stayed
3 too little
4 was arrested
5 asked (me) what I thought
6 don't/do not have to go
7 wish I hadn't/had not fallen
8 wish my boss would promote
9 don't/do not/wouldn't/would not
   mind teaching
10 if I'd/would like

🔧 Fix it notes

A Use *would prefer* + infinitive and *would rather* + base form to express preferences. Use the past simple and past perfect after *wish* to talk about present and past wishes. Use *would* + base form after *wish* to talk about the future. *If only* means the same as *I wish*.

B Use third conditional sentences to talk about things that have already happened in the past and their consequences. Use the past perfect in the *if*-clause and *would/wouldn't have* in the other clause.

C Use *enough* to say that there's as much of something as necessary. Use *too* to say that there's more than necessary. *Enough* goes after an adjective or adverb. *Too* goes before an adjective or adverb.

D Form the passive with an appropriate tense of the verb *be* + past participle. The subject of an active sentence becomes the object of a passive sentence.

E Report questions by putting auxiliary and modal verbs after (not before) the subject. Don't use *do*, *does* or *did*.

F Use *has/have to* in an appropriate tense to express obligation. Use *doesn't/don't have to* to express a lack of necessity. Use *don't mind* + *-ing* form or noun to say that you're willing to do something or happy about something.

For more information, see the
Review page opposite. ▷

ℹ Review

Would prefer/rather You use *would prefer* + infinitive and *would rather* + base form to express preferences.
I'd prefer to go to the theatre than the cinema.   I'd rather go to London by car than by train.

Wish and **if only** You use the past simple and past perfect after *wish* to talk about present and past wishes. You use *would* + base form after *wish* to talk about the future.
I wish I had more time. (present meaning = 'I don't have much time.')
I wish I hadn't been rude. (past meaning = 'I was rude.')

If only means the same as *I wish* but is more emphatic.
If only you hadn't crashed the car.

Third conditional You use third conditional sentences to talk about things that have already happened in the past and their consequences.
If you hadn't been late, we would have caught the train. (But we were late and we didn't catch the train.)

You use the past perfect in the *if*-clause of third conditional sentences and *would/wouldn't have* in the other clause.

⚠ Don't use *would have* in the *if*-clause.
I would have visited you if I had known you were ill.   NOT   *I would have visited you if I would have known you were ill.*

Too and **enough** You use *enough* to say that there's as much of something as necessary. You use *too* to say that there's more than necessary. *Enough* goes after an adjective or adverb. *Too* goes before an adjective or adverb.
You're not old enough to drive.
I'm too tired to go out.

You also use *too much/many* and *enough* before nouns.
There's too much salt in this dish.
You've bought too many vegetables.
We haven't got enough money to buy a new car.

The passive You form the passive with an appropriate tense of the verb *be* + past participle. The subject of an active sentence becomes the object of a passive sentence.
The children were invited to a party.

Reported questions You report questions by putting auxiliary and modal verbs after (not before) the subject. Don't use *do, does* or *did*.
Mum asked where I had been.
NOT   *Mum asked where had I been.*
The MD asked if I spoke French.
NOT   *The MD asked if I did speak French.*

Have to You use *has/have to* in an appropriate tense to express obligation. You use *doesn't/don't have to* to express a lack of necessity.
You'll have to get up early tomorrow.
You don't have to take the dog for a walk. I've already done it.

Don't mind You use *don't mind* + -ing form or noun to say that you're happy or willing to do something or happy about something.
I don't mind driving you to the station.
I don't mind the cold weather.

Error correction (4)

Test it ✔

① Find and cross out the unnecessary words.

I won't go out until you ~~will~~ get back.

a There are quite many reasons to eat organic food.
b Have you ever visited the Oxford University?
c Tom hasn't finished yet his homework.
d More relatives came to my wedding than I had expected them.
e Even although I like my job, I'd like a better one.
f Can you to help me with this little problem, please?
g Everyone managed to get to work even despite the snow.
h There's never enough of time to do all the things that need doing.
i By the time we will get there, the show will have started.
j Have you had already your breakfast?

② Choose the correct sentences.

	A	Can I to speak to Mr Eliot, please?	☒
	B	Tom's away now, but can I help you?	☑
a	A	I love Harry, so I'll follow him wherever he'll go.	☐
	B	I like my boyfriend so much that I'll follow him wherever he goes.	☐
b	A	Claire doesn't understand enough Spanish to speak it well.	☐
	B	She doesn't know enough of Spanish so she's going to do a course.	☐
c	A	There are enough of those tomatoes to make a salad.	☐
	B	You've eaten enough that cake already.	☐
d	A	The teacher said I must learn some past participles.	☐
	B	He said I must to learn some irregular verbs as well.	☐
e	A	Have you yet read the email Paddy sent?	☐
	B	Have you checked your emails yet?	☐
f	A	Bill looked quite tired when he came to stay with us.	☐
	B	There are quite many mistakes in your test, I'm afraid.	☐
g	A	Let's drive to London, then catch a train from the Waterloo station.	☐
	B	Waterloo station is where we catch the Eurostar to Brussels.	☐
h	A	Katrina had more friends than she realised.	☐
	B	Don't worry. We've got more time than I thought it.	☐
i	A	Although the weather was terrible, they had a good time.	☐
	B	Even in spite of the terrible weather, they had a good time.	☐
j	A	They built the Chartres Cathedral about eight centuries ago.	☐
	B	Chartres Cathedral was built about eight centuries ago.	☐

20

GO to page 80 and check your answers.

Test it again ✔

Read the text below and look carefully at each line. Some of the lines are correct, and some have a word which should not be there. If a line is correct, put a tick (✓) next to it. If a line has a word that should not be there, cross it out.

NEW YORK, NEW YORK

1   I travelled a lot as a child, which was lucky because I saw some great
2   sights, but it wasn't until much later that I appreciated them. Some places were
3   more interesting than I had imagined them. Others didn't really interest me
4   so much. I liked buildings most of all. The New York station, for example – who
5   could to imagine a more impressive building? It's a fine example
6   of architecture, even although it's just a railway station. Its real name is Grand
7   Central, and I have stood in Vanderbilt Hall quite many times listening and
8   watching the people running for trains. 'Have you read already
9   the report I sent your office?' one man says to another. 'Bye, honey, see you
10 later. Don't forget to call me when you will get to work,' a husband says to his
11 wife. To me, those conversations and the energy of the station were wonderful.
12 I remember visiting New York for the first time. My memory of the city
13 isn't very good but my mum kept a diary and I must to find it. Thinking
14 about New York makes me want to go back. There's so much yet I haven't seen,
15 like Union Square and the Met. If I go enough of times, it'll soon feel like home.

15

🔧 Fix it

Answers to Test it

Check your answers. Wrong answer?
Read the right Fix it note to find out why.

1 • you ~~will~~ get → F
  a are ~~quite~~ many → A
  b visited ~~the~~ Oxford → B
  c finished ~~yet~~ his → C
  d expected ~~them~~ → D
  e ~~Even~~ although → E
  f you ~~to~~ help → G
  g work ~~even~~ despite → E
  h enough ~~of~~ time → E
  i we ~~will~~ get → F
  j had ~~already~~ your → C

2 • B → G
  a B → F
  b A → E
  c A → E
  d A → G
  e B → C
  f A → A
  g B → B
  h A → D
  i A → E
  j B → B

Now go to page 79. Test yourself again.

Answers to Test it again

1 ✔	9 ✔
2 ✔	10 ~~will~~
3 ~~them~~	11 ✔
4 ~~The~~	12 ✔
5 ~~to~~	13 ~~to~~
6 ~~even~~	14 ~~yet~~
7 ~~quite~~	15 ~~of~~
8 ~~already~~	

🔧 Fix it notes

A Use *quite* with gradable adjectives, e.g. *tired, funny, well*. Don't use *quite + many +* noun. Use *quite a lot of* or *quite a few* instead.

B Don't use an article with the names of buildings and organizations which start with the name of a town, e.g. *Oxford University*.

C When you use the adverbs *already* and *just* with the present perfect, they go between the auxiliary and the past participle. *Yet* goes at the end of a sentence or clause.

D *Than* replaces subject and object pronouns so you don't need to repeat them.

E Don't put *even* before *although, despite* or *in spite of*. Use (*not +*) adjective/ adverb + *enough* + noun or infinitive. Before *a, the, his, this,* etc., you can use *enough of*. You don't usually use *of* + noun after *enough*.

F Use the present simple, not *will*, to talk about the future after these expressions: *by the time, when, after, until, before, wherever*.

G Use the base form, not the infinitive, after modal verbs, e.g. *can, could, must, should*.

> For more information, see the Review page opposite.

ⓘ Review

Quite Adjectives can be gradable, e.g. *tired, funny, good*, or non-gradable, e.g. *dead, unique, perfect*. You usually use *quite* with gradable adjectives. You only use *quite* with non-gradable adjectives when it means 'completely'.
I was quite tired last night. (= rather tired)
The story was quite untrue. (= completely untrue)

You don't use *quite* + *many* + noun. You use *quite a lot of* with uncountable nouns or *quite a few* with countable nouns instead.
There was quite a lot of litter.
There were quite a few people at the party.

Articles You don't use an article with the names of buildings and organizations which start with the name of a town, e.g. *Oxford University*.
We walked across London Bridge.
Let's meet at Heathrow Airport.

Already, just and yet When you use the adverbs *already* and *just* with the present perfect, they go between the auxiliary and the past participle. *Yet* goes at the end of a sentence or clause.
We've already had lunch.
The train has just left.
The children haven't come back from school yet.
Have you finished your exams yet?

Than In sentences with *more than*, the word *than* replaces subject and object pronouns so you don't need to repeat them.
The flights cost much more than I had expected. NOT *The flights cost much more than I had expected it.*

Even Don't confuse *even though* and *although*. You don't put *even* before *although, despite* or *in spite of*.
We arrived on time although the traffic was very heavy. OR *We arrived on time even though the traffic was very heavy.*

There was a huge crowd at the match in spite of/despite the heavy rain.
NOT *There was a huge crowd at the match even in spite of/despite the heavy rain.*

Enough (of) You use (*not* +) adjective/ adverb + *enough* + noun or infinitive. Before *a, the, his, this*, etc., you can use *enough of*. You can use *enough* + noun but you don't usually use *of* + noun after *enough*.
I didn't revise carefully enough for the test.
You aren't old enough to join the army.
Have you had enough cake? OR *Have you had enough of this cake?* NOT *Have you had enough this cake?*

Present simple You use the present simple, not *will*, to talk about the future after these expressions: *by the time, when, after, until, before, wherever*.
By the time we get home, it will be dark.
We'll go for a drink when I see you next week. Let's have a pizza after the film finishes. Please wait until the bus stops before you get off. Whenever Ms Lee arrives, please let me know.

Modal verbs Modal verbs include *can, could, must, may, might, should*, etc. You use the base form (not the infinitive) after modal verbs, e.g. *can, could, must*.
You should see the doctor soon.
NOT *You should to see the doctor soon.*

Word formation (4)

Test it ✔

1 Complete the sentences. Use the correct form of the words in brackets, in the correct order.

The teacher said we were ...*annoying*............ and the noise from our class was
ᵃ............................. and that she would make a ᵇ............................. to the head if
we continued to ᶜ............................. . (behave / complain / annoy / bear)

My driving ᵈ............................. advised me to be ᵉ............................. when out in
the hours of ᶠ............................. . (dark / caution / instruct)

The stamp ᵍ............................. thought that her collection was ʰ............................. ,
so she said that the valuation at £50,000 was beyond ⁱ.......... . (believe / worth /
collect)

2 Look at the words in bold and correct any mistakes.

	My diary was ruined in the storm. It's **unuseable** now.	....*unusable*..........
a	I was so worried that I spent several **sleepless** nights.	....
b	Why do you always **misunderstand** what I say?	....
c	The weather in this region is never **predictible**.	....
d	It's **surprising** to see how things have changed here.	....
e	Do you think that snake is **poisoning**?	....
f	Ed never wins at golf, but he's a good **competiter**.	....
g	The **brighten** of the sun in Greece was just incredible.	....
h	The job requires good **knowledge** of overseas markets.	....
i	We live in quite a **mountained** region.	....
j	Can you measure the **length** of this skirt for me?	....
k	How **ambitious** are you?	....

20

GO to page 84 and check your answers.

Test it again ✔

Read the text below. Use the word given in capitals at the end of each line to form a word that fits in the space in the same line.

THE LANGUAGE INSTINCT

When I was young, I found language classes rather (1)..... I enjoyed **POINT**
other subjects, but languages were my (2)..... I couldn't understand **WEAK**
a word and I used to (3).... everything. My teachers knew I was an **PRONOUNCE**
(4).... student who wanted to do well, but I let myself down in **AMBITION**
languages. My marks were (5).... in French and German and I wanted **ACCEPT**
to give up. Then one year I went to Germany and something (6).... **AMAZE**
happened. It all started to make sense. I took (7).... in talking **PROUD**
to people. I didn't feel like a (8).... any more and I started **FAIL**
to make progress. In fact, languages became one of my (9)...... **STRONG**
I went on to study German at college and became a good (10)...... **COMMUNICATE**

1 POINT .... 6 AMAZE ....

2 WEAK .... 7 PROUD ....

3 PRONOUNCE .... 8 FAIL ....

4 AMBITION .... 9 STRONG ....

5 ACCEPT .... 10 COMMUNICATE ....

20

🔧 Fix it

Answers to Test it

Check your answers. Wrong answer?
Read the right Fix it note to find out why.

1 • annoying → G
  a unbearable → D
  b complaint → H
  c misbehave → C
  d instructor → B
  e cautious → F
  f darkness → E
  g collector → B
  h worthless → A
  i belief → H

2 • unusable → D
  a correct → A
  b correct → C
  c predictable → D
  d correct → G
  e poisonous → F
  f competitor → B
  g brightness → E
  h correct → H
  i mountainous → F
  j correct → H
  k correct → F

Now go to page 83. Test yourself again.

Answers to Test it again

1 pointless
2 weakness/weaknesses
3 mispronounce
4 ambitious
5 unacceptable
6 amazing
7 pride
8 failure
9 strengths
10 communicator

🔧 Fix it notes

A To make a negative adjective from some nouns, add -less, e.g. hope → hopeless.

B To make a personal noun from some verbs, add -or, e.g. object → objector. You sometimes need to make changes to the base verb, e.g. communicate → communicator, compete → competitor.

C To make some verbs negative, add mis-, e.g. behave → misbehave.

D To make an adjective from some verbs to give the meaning 'can be done', add -able, e.g. employ → employable. You can add prefixes to some of these adjectives to make the meaning negative, e.g. unemployable.

E To make a noun from some adjectives, add -ness, e.g. dark → darkness, bright → brightness.

F To make an adjective from some nouns, use -ous, e.g. caution → cautious.

G To make a present participle that can be used as an adjective from some verbs, add -ing, e.g. surprise → surprising.

H Some words do not add prefixes or suffixes to make new words. These are less predictable changes and it's best to learn them as you go along, e.g. believe → belief, long → length.

> For more information, see the Review page opposite. ▷

ⓘ Review

- To prepare for this part of the test, it's useful to record vocabulary in word 'families', e.g. *own, disown, owner, ownership.*
- Make sure you know what different prefixes and suffixes mean and keep a record of these in a vocabulary notebook.

See page 86 for a description of this part of the Use of English paper.

Suffix *-less* You can make a negative adjective from some nouns by adding the suffix *-less.*
hope ➔ hopeless
effort ➔ effortless
harm ➔ harmless

Suffix *-or* You can make a personal noun from some verbs by adding *-or.*
object ➔ objector
act ➔ actor
connect ➔ connector

You sometimes need to make changes to the base verb.
communicate ➔ communicator
compete ➔ competitor

Prefix *mis-* You can make some verbs negative by adding *mis-.*
behave ➔ misbehave
calculate ➔ miscalculate
hear ➔ mishear

Suffix *-able* To make an adjective from some verbs to give the meaning 'can be done', you can add *-able.*
accept ➔ acceptable
employ ➔ employable
record ➔ recordable

You can also add prefixes to some of these adjectives to make the meaning negative, e.g. *unemployable, unacceptable.* See Word formation (1) on page 25 for more information on opposite adjectives.

Suffix *-ness* You can make a noun from some adjectives by adding *-ness.*
dark ➔ darkness
bright ➔ brightness

Suffix *-ous* You can make an adjective from some nouns by using the suffix *-ous.*
caution ➔ cautious
ambition ➔ ambitious
infection ➔ infectious

Present participles as adjectives You can make a present participle from some verbs and use them as adjectives by adding *-ing* to the base verb.
surprise ➔ surprising
bore ➔ boring
frighten ➔ frightening

Other types of word formation With some words, you can't add prefixes or suffixes to make new words. These are less predictable changes and it's best to learn the words as you go along.
arrive ➔ arrival
know ➔ knowledge

The FCE Use of English Paper

There are five parts to the FCE Use of English paper (paper 3) and you have one hour and fifteen minutes to complete them. Here are some guidelines to help you perform well in the exam.

1 Divide the time across the five sections and leave yourself enough time for checking and transferring your answers to the answer sheet.
2 If you're unsure of an answer, leave it and come back to it at the end.
3 Make sure you record your answers on the answer sheet accurately. You must use a pencil.
4 Try to be sure about your answers before you transfer them to the answer sheet. If you make a mistake on the answer sheet, rub it out carefully and make your correction clearly.
5 Make sure your handwriting is clear and that your spelling is correct when you write the answers on the answer sheet.
6 Don't leave any blanks – guess if you're not sure. You won't lose marks for wrong answers.

Here's a brief description of what you need to do in each part of paper 3.

Part 1: multiple-choice cloze
15 questions, one mark each

In part 1, you read a text with 15 gaps and choose from four options (A–D) to complete the text. The focus of this task is mainly on vocabulary, but the answer you choose needs to fit both the meaning and the grammar of the sentence. Part 1 includes words that have similar meanings, e.g. *rob* and *steal*; collocations, e.g. *accept responsibility*; phrasal verbs, e.g. *put up*; linking words, e.g. *but, as*; prepositional phrases, e.g. *as for, because of*, and fixed expressions, e.g. *make money, go to school*.

Part 2: open cloze
15 questions, one mark each

In part 2, you also read a text with 15 gaps but this time you write one word in each gap. The focus of this task is grammar and vocabulary. The missing words are often grammatical ones, but may also be part of a phrase or expression. The words may be articles e.g. *a, the*; prepositions, e.g. *on, in*; linking words e.g. *unless, despite*; pronouns e.g. *that, which*; comparatives, e.g. *more, most*; parts of phrasal verbs, e.g. *give up, run out of*; auxiliary verbs, e.g. *had, can*; quantifiers, e.g. *a lot of, several*, and determiners, e.g. *both, neither*.

Part 3: key word transformations
10 questions, one mark each

In part 3, you rewrite 10 sentences using a given word. This task focuses on grammar and vocabulary and the language tested may include: grammatical patterns, auxiliary verbs, phrasal verbs, reported speech, passive forms, 'unreal' past, gerunds and infinitives, modal verbs, verb tenses, comparisons, conditionals, changing from a noun to a verb structure and vice versa.

Part 4: error correction
15 questions, one mark each

In part 4, you read a text with 15 numbered lines. The text is often the type of writing a student might do, and so it may look like part of a letter or an email. You decide if the lines in the text contain an extra word that shouldn't be there. Between two and five lines will be correct. The extra words are usually grammatical words: auxiliary verbs, e.g. *do, has*; prepositions, e.g. *up, at*; articles, e.g. *a, an, the*; pronouns, e.g. *them, what*; determiners, e.g. *this, every*; quantifiers, e.g. *some, many*, and comparatives, e.g. *more interesting, most expensive*. Note that this task can also cover word order, negative forms, e.g. *not, never*, and phrasal verbs.

Part 5: word formation
10 questions, one mark each

In part 5, you read a text with 10 gaps, one in each line. There is a word in capitals at the end of each line. You use these words to form new words to complete the text, e.g. adjectives from nouns, verbs from adjectives. You may need to add prefixes, suffixes and make internal changes to the words. Be careful! Sometimes you have to make more than one change to form the new word. You also need to spell the new word correctly.

List of grammatical structures

In this book, you are tested on a large number of grammatical structures. For more detailed practice and explanation of some of these, see the corresponding units in *Test it, Fix it Grammar for FCE*.

Page numbers shown refer to *Test it, Fix it Grammar for FCE*.

Spelling in English

Capital letters

Use capital letters for the following categories of word:

People's names and names of places
Patrick, London, Japan

Nationalities
Belgian, Greek, Irish

All days, months and official holidays
Saturday, June, Easter

Doubling the final consonant of words

You often need to double the final consonant of a word when you add *-ed, -ing, -er, -es*. Here are some common examples:

Double the final *b, d, g, l, m, n, p, r* and *t* at the end of words.
sob → sobbing; sad → sadder; big → bigger; travel → traveller; swim → swimming; thin → thinner; hop → hopping; refer → referred; sit → sitting

If you see a consonant, vowel, consonant pattern at the end of a word, also double the final letter.
admit → admitted

Only double the final letter of words with more than one syllable when the final syllable is stressed.
begin - beginning

Words that end in *e*

When you're forming a new word by adding a suffix that begins with a vowel to a word that ends in *e*, you usually need to take away the *e* and add the suffix.
make → making; shine → shining

Be careful! Leave the final *e* if the word ends in *-ee, -ge,* or *-ce.*
agree → agreeable; encourage → encouragement; change → changeable

Words that end in *y*

When you're forming a new word by adding a suffix, you usually change the *y* to an *i.*
happy → happiness; pretty → prettily; funny → funnily

Also change a final *y* to an *i* when you make a countable noun plural.
dictionary → dictionaries; party → parties; curry → curries

Make the same change for the third person singular of verbs which end in *y.*
cry → cries; hurry → hurries

However, note that you don't change the *y* to an *i* when there's a vowel before the *y.*
stay → stays; enjoy → enjoyed

Be careful! There are some exceptions.
say → said; lay → laid; pay → paid

ie or *ei*?

You usually put *i* before *e.*
friend, believe, achieve

There are some exceptions to the '*i* before *e*' rule.
weird, their, seize, ceiling, receipt, perceive, receive, deceive, neighbour, weight, height, either, neither, foreign, leisure